Geek the Library: A Community Awareness Campaign

A Report to the OCLC Membership

Geek the Library: A Community Awareness Campaign

A Report to the OCLC Membership

Principal contributors

Cathy De Rosa, Vice President for the Americas and Global Vice President of Marketing

Jenny Johnson, Executive Director, Branding and Marketing Services

Linn Haugestad Edvardsen, Senior Editor

Patricia Harris, Field Consultant

Graphics, layout and editing

Brad Gauder, Editor

Matt Carlson, Senior Designer

Rick Limes, Art Director

Research partner

Leo Burnett USA

OCLC would like to thank:

The Bill & Melinda Gates Foundation for funding the pilot campaign and the research presented in this report.

Mary Wegner, State Librarian of Iowa

Dr. Lamar Veatch, State Librarian of Georgia

The support staff of both the Georgia Public Library Service and the State Library of Iowa for their helpful efforts on behalf of the Geek the Library campaign.

The administration and staff of the public libraries involved in the Geek the Library pilot campaign for their commitment of time and resources, their creativity and enthusiasm, and their insightful feedback throughout the project.

OCLC
Dublin, Ohio USA

Copyright © 2011, OCLC Online Computer Library Center, Inc.
6565 Kilgour Place
Dublin, Ohio 43017-3395

ALL RIGHTS RESERVED. No part of this publication may be reproduced, stored in a retrieval system or transmitted, in any form or by any means, electronic, mechanical, photocopying or otherwise, without prior written permission of the copyright holder.

The following are trademarks and/or service marks of OCLC: OCLC, the OCLC logo, Geek the Library, What Do You Geek? and Get Your Geek On.

Third-party product, service, business and other proprietary names are trademarks and/or service marks of their respective owners.

Printed in the United States of America

Cataloged in WorldCat on December 13, 2010
OCLC Control Number: 692197509

ISBN: 1-55653-393-4
     978-1-55653-393-8

16 15 14 13 12 11 | 1 2 3 4 5 6

Table of Contents

	Chapter/Page
Introduction	**vii**
Executive Summary	**xi**
The Geek the Library Theory	**1-1**
Geek the Library: A Pilot	**2-1**
Geek the Library Delivers	**3-1**
Geek the Library in Action	**4-1**
Get Geek the Library	**5-1**
Appendices	
A: Glossary	A-1
B: List of Pilot Libraries	B-1
C: About Our Partners	C-1
D: About OCLC	D-1

Introduction

From concept to reality

In 2007, we embarked on a national research project to test the hypothesis that the emerging U.S. public library funding crisis could be improved by implementing large-scale community awareness campaigns aimed at engaging and educating the public library's current and potential supporters. In the three years that our research has been underway, the funding crisis for U.S. public libraries has gone from an emerging issue to an emergency issue. The U.S. economic situation has created urgent, and growing, demand for library services. The 'What if?' library funding scenarios we explored with our focus group participants in 2007 have become reality. Libraries have been closed. Hours have been cut. Funding has declined. The 2007 'What if?' research questions have become the 2011 'What now?' or 'What next?' library management questions.

So, does our 2007 hypothesis still hold in the new, harsher U.S. economic environment? Is it possible to improve the potential for increased library funding through stronger library marketing, educational efforts and advocacy in this tough economy? Our recent field trial of the Geek the Library community awareness campaign suggests that the answer to that question is: "Yes!"

During 2009 and 2010, we piloted the campaign with nearly 100 libraries in test markets in southern Georgia and central Iowa, and in additional communities in Georgia, Illinois, Indiana and Wisconsin. Our goal was to test the validity of the three primary funding marketing imperatives identified in the 2007 quantitative research.

A successful community awareness campaign has to do three things:

1. Wake up potential supporters to the fact that the library is relevant in the 21st century

2. Put libraries squarely in the mix of important community infrastructure, alongside fire, police and schools

3. Activate conversations about the vital and transformative role that the library plays, and its value to the community.

The research also told us that the potential supporters we need to wake up and activate with our awareness campaigns are not necessarily our library users. Changing the funding cycle for libraries requires new, bolder campaigns and conversations aimed squarely at the segment of our communities who see, or could see, the library as a source of transformation, not simply as a source of information. Our long-held marketing assumptions about understanding library user demographics or life stages, and crafting our message to match these users' needs, is just not sufficient.

Library support is an attitude, not a demographic. Therefore, a successful awareness campaign has to be a community-based educational effort, not an in-library initiative aimed at users. We have to take our message to the streets, to the parks, to city councils, to our schools, to our businesses, to our farmers markets, to our Rotary clubs, to our bus shelters, to our airports and beyond. If we want to wake up the potential supporters, we first have to get their attention.

I geek superheroes, I geek vampires, I geek composting and I geek jobs.

What do you geek?

This may not be a question you might expect from a community awareness campaign, but it is just the type of question needed to grab a potential library supporter's attention. It is also the type of question that can start a different type of library dialogue. Not a discussion of library programs, but rather a conversation about community passions, transformative actions and the ability of the public library to help transform lives—no matter what our residents need or what they "geek."

Geek the Library was crafted by our advertising partner Leo Burnett USA, but it was brought to life by the talented and terrific staffs of the pilot libraries. The campaign activities and ideas you will see and read about in the pilot results that follow are absolutely amazing. The staff embraced the challenge and took the message of the transformational value of the library into the community and to the potential supporters. And they saw results.

Market surveys conducted before and after the pilot campaigns, and the feedback from the participating library leaders and staff, provide strong evidence that an awareness campaign aimed at telling the library story can drive change. During the first months that the campaign pilot was in the test markets, the campaign reached over half of the more than one million residents in our pilot communities. Perceptions of the libraries as a source of importance support for the community increased, and more residents felt it was important to support their public library. Most importantly, the campaign generated action. Over two-thirds of the residents who saw the campaign took action or intended to take action. This included talking with family and friends, visiting the library or the geekthelibrary.org Web site, volunteering or donating time or money to the library.

The pilot libraries made the difference. I would like to thank the hundreds of librarians who "got their geek on" for the pilot campaign and tested dozens of ideas. They devoted weekends and evenings, and weathered the sun, rain and crowds to take the library message to the community—thank you all for the invaluable learning that you have provided!

A special thanks to the staff and leadership at our hub libraries, Live Oak Public Libraries and Des Moines Public Library, for their dedication to the project; and to Mary Wegner, State Librarian of Iowa, and Dr. Lamar Veatch, State Librarian of Georgia, for their continued support. And finally, a very special thanks to the Bill & Melinda Gates Foundation—specifically Jill Nishi, Deputy Director of U.S. Libraries and Special Initiatives for the foundation—for its funding and support of this campaign, and for its ongoing dedication to helping libraries.

This pilot, of course, is just the start—a brief test of what could be possible from a long-term, wide-scale community awareness effort. So, we invite you to take the campaign and put it into action in your community. The program—the campaign materials, ideas and lessons learned—is free and available to any U.S. public library. Chapter 5 tells you more about how you can get started. Please visit get.geekthelibrary.org to learn more.

Sincerely,

Cathy De Rosa
Vice President for the Americas and
Global Vice President of Marketing
OCLC

I geek library funding.

Executive Summary

Geek the Library makes an impact

Geek the Library gets people talking about libraries and library funding.

Geek the Library's bold look attracts attention and its simple message helps make a very personal connection to the library. This community awareness campaign provides a light-hearted approach to a very serious message. The campaign focuses on educating the public about the value of the library and the critical funding challenges many libraries face while asking the public what they "geek"—what they are passionate about.

Created by OCLC with research partner Leo Burnett USA and funded by a grant from the Bill & Melinda Gates Foundation, Geek the Library illustrates the fact that everyone is passionate about something—everyone "geeks" something—and that the public library supports it all. The campaign includes advertising, marketing, public relations, community events, a campaign Web site, social media and other online tools.

The campaign was piloted from June 2009 to April 2010 with nearly 100 public libraries in southern Georgia and central Iowa, as well as additional communities in Georgia, Illinois, Indiana and Wisconsin. Geek the Library helped participants educate the public about the value of the library and library funding, and start important local conversations about the library. The campaign encouraged residents to think differently about the library—not only as relevant and necessary, but also hip and cool, and transformational.

The Geek the Library pilot campaign was a success! Qualitative and quantitative research before and after the pilot, as well as stories from participating libraries, provide proof that the campaign can help library leaders and staff make a positive impact on changing public perceptions about the library and library funding.

The Geek the Library story

In 2005, the library community recognized a troubling, downward public library funding trend occurring across the United States. Overall, funding was not keeping pace with growing circulation and library visits, and increasing demand for resources. Federal and state funding had flattened or declined, and many libraries reported difficulty raising funds from local sources. Other locally funded services also faced economic challenges and competition for local resources.

Many libraries understood the need to put effort into advocacy programs to increase awareness of the issue, but with so many demands on their resources, it was often difficult to create and implement such a program. OCLC developed a theory that a community-centered public awareness campaign—one that uses strategies similar to those of many successful brands and focuses on funding awareness, not usage—could be implemented on a broad scale and make an impact locally. But what groups of people would the campaign need to reach and what would the campaign message include?

With a grant from the Bill & Melinda Gates Foundation, OCLC partnered with Leo Burnett USA and conducted an extensive consumer study in 2007. The goal of the research was twofold: first, to understand the factors that drive, and limit, local library funding support; and second, to ascertain whether a large-scale library support campaign could be effective at increasing and sustaining funding for U.S. public libraries by reaching and influencing the segments of the voting population that have the most potential to become committed library supporters.

Quantitative research identified specific segments of the population more apt to support library funding. The segmentation analysis identified four categories, with two being vital to the success of any community awareness campaign:

- **Probable Supporters:** These voters are likely to support library funding initiatives, but are not fully committed. Since their vote is not a given, Probable Supporters are the primary target of the Geek the Library campaign.

- **Super Supporters:** These are people who are most firmly committed to supporting a library funding initiative. Super Supporters are not the primary target for the campaign, but are important to mobilize to help spread the message and improve campaign impact.

Further analysis of the qualitative study findings helped produce a deeper understanding of factors influencing library support and perceptions. Some important findings:

- Most people claim that they would support the library at the ballot box—fewer are firmly committed to doing so.

- There is a lot that people don't know about their public libraries.

- Library support is only marginally related to visitation.

- Perceptions of the librarian are highly related to support.

- The library occupies a very clear position in people's minds as a provider of practical answers and information.

- Belief that the library is a transformational force in people's lives is directly related to their level of funding support.

- Increasing support for libraries may not necessarily mean a trade-off with financial support for other public services.

Additional qualitative research tested possible awareness campaign messages that were developed based on these findings. The results—documented in *From Awareness to Funding: A study of library support in America*—were clear: it could work.

Public libraries pilot the campaign

The research findings informed development of the Geek the Library community awareness campaign. The pilot campaign's objectives were to reposition the library as vital and relevant, and bring new life to its community standing. The personal message helped break through the marketing clutter and got people talking. Feedback from pilot libraries confirmed that the concept, while simple, had the potential to make considerable impact. The campaign's core message—everyone has something they are passionate about, something they geek and the library supports it all—resonated with a large percentage of the public in pilot communities.

Two regional areas, central Iowa and southern Georgia, were selected as pilot markets in June 2009, including 80 participating libraries. A small number of additional libraries were added at the end of 2009: Milwaukee Public Library in Wisconsin; Piedmont Regional Library System in Georgia (covering Banks, Barrow and Jackson Counties); Shelbyville-Shelby County Public Library in Shelbyville, Indiana; and Zion-Benton Public Library in Zion, Illinois. The official pilot campaign concluded in April 2010.

Even with increasing demands on their resources, participating library directors, managers and staff found time to effectively promote the awareness campaign to their local communities. Continuous feedback from these passionate advocates helped refine the program, and their creativity and enthusiasm provided many ideas to make the campaign stronger.

A combination of pilot library tracking components, feedback from the field, and online and offline tracking of specific campaign elements—as well as quantitative research that tracked statistical changes in public awareness and perceptions—form the results of the pilot campaign. The goal was to evaluate the effectiveness of the campaign to:

- **Raise awareness** about the campaign and the need for library support

- **Change attitudes and perceptions** about the library, the librarian and the need for increased library funding

- **Drive behavior** that relates to increasing support for the local library.

Outstanding results

The collective data provides many positive impact indicators. Geek the Library:

- **Got people's attention:** After five months, 64 percent of residents in central Iowa and 49 percent of residents in southern Georgia were familiar with the campaign.

- **Raised awareness:** Perceptions and attitudes around the library's importance and value in the community improved in southern Georgia, and more people said they were willing to fund the library.

- **Encouraged action:** More than two-thirds of residents in both southern Georgia and central Iowa had responded or intended to respond to the campaign in one or more ways, such as visiting the campaign Web site or telling a friend.

Positive results in all pilot markets can be attributed, in part, to a multipronged marketing approach that included advertising, public relations activities, community events, educational efforts and engagement with influential members of the community, such as public officials and the media.

The public was encouraged to interact with the campaign on the official Web site (geekthelibrary.org) where they could learn more about the campaign and funding, share what they geek, take part in a poll and sign up for e-mail updates. Over the course of the pilot campaign, hundreds of people shared what they geeked. People also embraced the social networking element of the campaign, showing particular interest on the Geek the Library Facebook page, which grew by over 13,000 fans during the campaign period and continues to add new fans.

Pilot library leaders and staff successfully initiated important funding conversations—a key objective of the campaign—by taking Geek the Library out into the community. Local events were an important element, and pilot library participants found creative ways to educate and engage the public. Library participants localized their campaigns using relevant local information in displays and handouts, and actively encouraged the public to take part by making personalized posters, connecting with Geek the Library online and spreading the word. Libraries also partnered with local schools, businesses and organizations to ensure as much of the community as possible participated in the campaign.

Available for U.S. public libraries

Pilot library leaders and staff went above and beyond program expectations and became vocal community advocates, and OCLC is extremely thankful for their efforts and support.

What began as a theory was proved to have impact in local communities and has reached far beyond the campaign's pilot markets. The campaign found a consumer and library following that represents people all over the United States. Interest in Geek the Library came from all over the world, including libraries in Australia, Sweden and Zimbabwe.

It is our hope that the experiences and learnings described in this report inspire other U.S. public libraries to adopt the awareness campaign and ask their communities to "geek" their library. Geek the Library is now open to all U.S. public libraries. Free materials, training and ongoing support are available. Interested libraries can visit get.geekthelibrary.org for more information.

The Geek the Library Theory

Chapter 1

We geek research

The comprehensive research study *From Awareness to Funding: A study of library support in America* found that increasing funding support for public libraries requires changing perceptions about public libraries from an institution that provides information to a critical piece of the community infrastructure that provides transformational opportunities.

This chapter features a recap of the study, including an overview of the library support segmentation, and the library funding drivers and supporter attitudes—all of which helped inform development of the strategy and creative approach for the Geek the Library community awareness campaign.

Defining the challenge

Public libraries face a deepening challenge. Most U.S. public libraries report increased traffic—especially for computers and Internet access. The need for resources to help people find jobs and reeducate themselves is at an all-time high. Over 25 million Americans used public libraries more than 20 times in 2009, up from 20.3 million in 2006.[1] Over 50 percent of U.S. public libraries reported flat or decreased operating budgets in fiscal year 2010—with many anticipating further cuts.[2] Increasing competition for local funding has also led to chronic budget cuts for many tax-supported community services over the past few years.

The Geek the Library community awareness campaign pilot project was born out of the need to bridge the gap between increasing public library usage and diminishing budgets. The campaign provides an effective way for libraries to improve support, and grow awareness and mindshare in their local communities. Most U.S. residents cannot describe how their local library is funded and they are unaware that the majority of funding for U.S. public library operations comes from local tax receipts.

The campaign design, strategy and implementation were informed by the research findings of an advocacy research grant awarded to OCLC by the Bill & Melinda Gates Foundation. The detailed research findings are documented in the 2008 OCLC membership report, *From Awareness to Funding: A study of library support in America*.

The research: an overview

The viability of a large-scale advocacy campaign to create an environment to sustain and increase funding for U.S. public libraries was put to the test. The goal of the research project was twofold: to understand the factors that drive, and limit, local library funding support; and to ascertain whether a national library support campaign could be effective at increasing and sustaining funding for U.S. public libraries by reaching and influencing the segments of the voting population that have the most potential to become committed library supporters.

---

1. American Library Association, "Libraries: Getting America Back to Work, A Legislative Proposal to Save Libraries and Help Job Seekers," http://www.ala.org/ala/aboutala/offices/wo/libraryjobs.pdf.
2. American Library Association, "Libraries Connect Communities: Public Library Funding & Technology Access Study 2009-2010," http://www.ala.org/ala/research/initiatives/plftas/2009_2010/index.cfm#final%20report.

Research hypothesis

U.S. public libraries face similar marketing and advocacy challenges to those endured by other super brands. Lessons learned and successes achieved can be applied to increase library funding. Utilizing marketing and advocacy techniques targeted to the right community segments with the right messages and community programs, we can improve the state of public library funding.

The research was designed to test the application of traditional market research, segmentation and targeting techniques to the library funding problem.

Research objectives

- To create a market segmentation analysis of the U.S. voting population that identified which segments of voters are most likely to generate increased support for U.S. public libraries, and to uncover underlying library motivations and attitudes that are indicative and predictive of the level of support for library funding.

- To understand the attitudes and behaviors of elected and appointed officials about libraries in general, the library's importance to the community, and how those attitudes impact the officials' willingness to support local library funding.

Research methodology

The quantitative study targeted two audiences: U.S. residents in communities with populations of less than 200,000 and elected officials in the United States. The study was intentionally designed to capture and analyze the attitudes, behaviors and opinions of residents in these communities. The quantitative survey provided data across a sample of 1,901 adults. The survey data for the total sample have a statistical margin of error of +/− 2.4 percentage points at the 95 percent confidence level for the U.S. population ages 18–69 in communities of less than 200,000 people.

Additionally, two rounds of qualitative research were conducted to understand the attitudes and perceptions of the voters identified during the quantitative research as the most likely supporters. The qualitative research was also used to test messaging for a potential library support campaign. The research, published in *From Awareness to Funding: A study of library support in America*, indicated that an advocacy campaign targeting the appropriate audience with the right message could have significant impact on support for local library funding.

Creating a library support segmentation

Much like other brands, public libraries face the challenge of creating an effective message, identifying the appropriate audiences, and changing perceptions in a way that might impact current and future behavior related to library support. Using a robust market segmentation methodology, the survey data were analyzed to create a Library Supporter Segmentation framework that categorizes and profiles segments of the voting population in relation to their level of commitment to public library funding support.

The segmentation analysis identified six constructs that are the key drivers of library funding attitudes and behaviors:

- Likelihood of voting favorably if a library referendum is on the ballot
- General voting behavior
- Stated barriers to using or supporting the library
- The library services they use
- Overall attitudes toward the library
- Perceptions of librarians

Library funding support is not driven by demographics, such as income, age, gender, race, political affiliation, etc. Voters' attitudes, perceptions and behaviors, not their demographic profiles, are the most important determinants of willingness to support increases in library funding. Library support is more about a mindset or an attitude than a traditional demographic profile.

A Library Supporter Segmentation Pyramid was developed based on the six identified constructs. Library supporters were categorized from those least likely to fund libraries at the ballot box (those at the bottom of the pyramid) to those most likely to vote in favor of a library referendum (those at the top of the pyramid).

Understanding, leveraging and delivering the appropriate message to these segments is a vital element of any successful awareness campaign. These findings provide the foundation for the strategy and the structure of Geek the Library.

Library Supporter Segmentation Pyramid

Total respondents

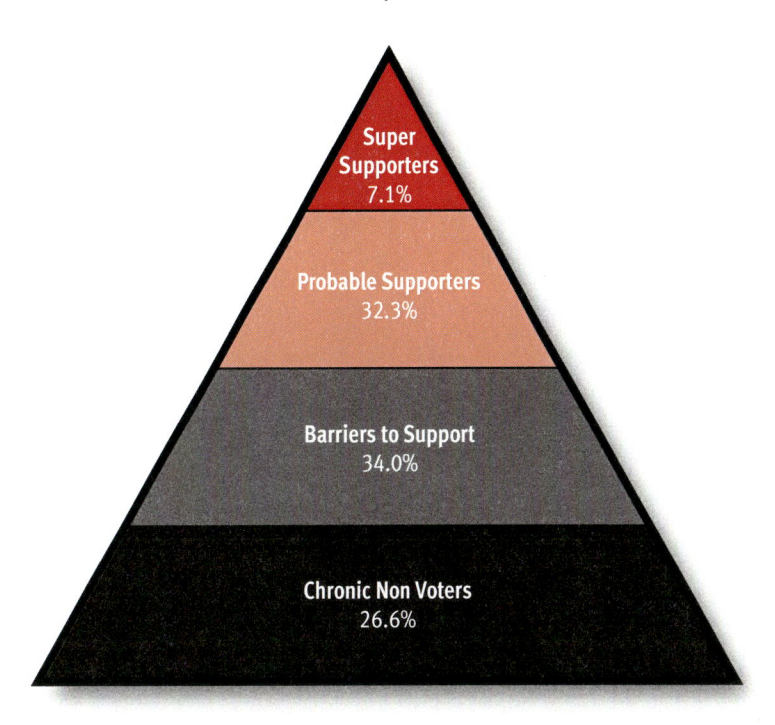

- Super Supporters 7.1%
- Probable Supporters 32.3%
- Barriers to Support 34.0%
- Chronic Non Voters 26.6%

Population ages 18–69 living in communities of less than 200,000 U.S. residents.
Source: *From Awareness to Funding*, OCLC, 2008

The segmentation pyramid identified four distinct tiers:

- **Super Supporters:** Voters at the top tier of the segmentation pyramid. These are people who are most firmly committed to supporting a library funding initiative.

- **Probable Supporters:** Voters who are likely to support library funding initiatives, but are not fully committed.

- **Barriers to Support:** Voters who, for a variety of factors, have significant barriers to voting in favor of increased library funding.

- **Chronic Non Voters:** People who are not registered to vote or have a history of choosing not to vote in national and local elections.

Analysis of the middle two tiers identified variations and characteristics that were unique enough to merit further market segmentation. The Barriers to Support tier included three segments described as Financially Strapped, Detached and The Web Wins. The Probable Supporter tier was made up of five segments: Just for Fun, Kid Driven, Library as Office, Look to Librarians and Greater Good.

Library Supporter Segmentation Pyramid

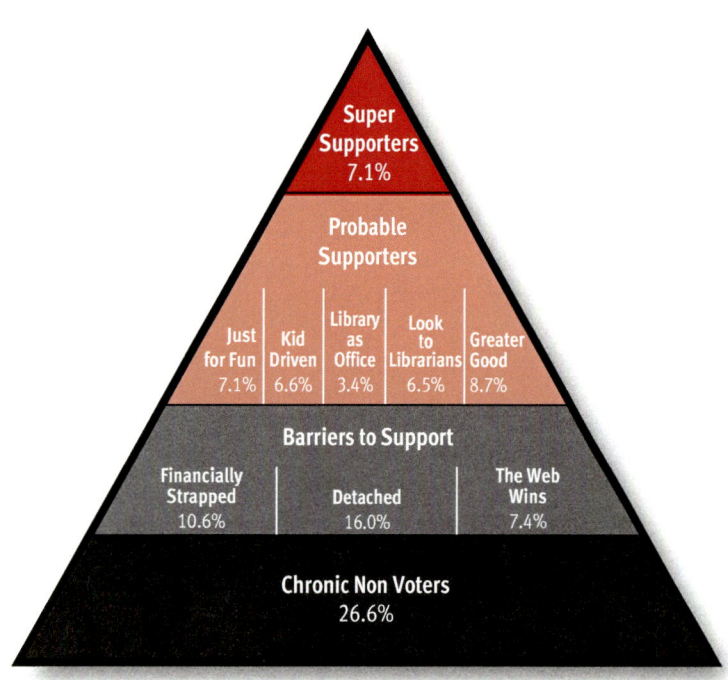

Total respondents

- **Super Supporters** 7.1%
- **Probable Supporters**
  - Just for Fun 7.1%
  - Kid Driven 6.6%
  - Library as Office 3.4%
  - Look to Librarians 6.5%
  - Greater Good 8.7%
- **Barriers to Support**
  - Financially Strapped 10.6%
  - Detached 16.0%
  - The Web Wins 7.4%
- **Chronic Non Voters** 26.6%

Percentage of population ages 18–69 living in communities of less than 200,000 U.S. residents.
Source: *From Awareness to Funding*, OCLC, 2008

Identifying library funding drivers

The quantitative survey identified a number of factors that drive, and limit, funding support of U.S. public libraries. These include information about the attitudes and behaviors of the respondents related to libraries, librarians, the library's role in the community, and respondents' willingness to increase taxes to support funding for libraries and other locally funded public services.

- **Most people claimed they would support the library at the ballot box—fewer are firmly committed to it.** Respondents were asked about their intent to vote if there was a library referendum, ballot initiative or bond measure during the next local election. A large percentage of respondents claimed they would either probably vote yes, or definitely vote yes, to increase funding for their local public library. After eliminating the respondents who were not registered to vote or showed a track record of not voting (identified as Chronic Non Voters), almost three quarters of the remaining voting respondents (74 percent) claimed that they would either probably or definitely vote yes; this group was evenly split with 37 percent saying they would probably vote yes for a library referendum and 37 percent saying they would definitely vote yes.

Only 37% of voters say that they would *definitely* support the library at the ballot box

Total voting respondents

Respondents were asked: If there was a referendum, ballot initiative or bond measure for your local public library on the ballot, how do you think you would vote?

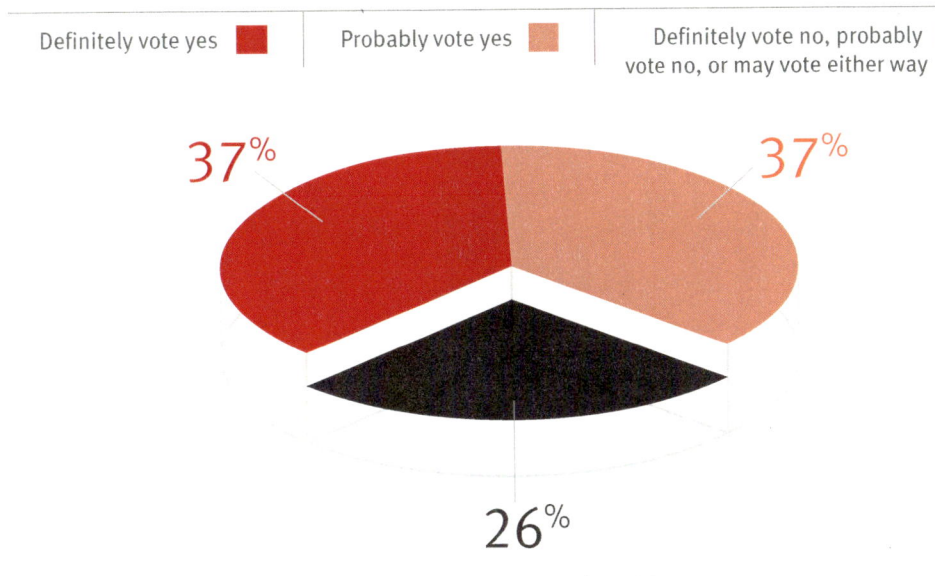

Definitely vote yes ■ | Probably vote yes ■ | Definitely vote no, probably vote no, or may vote either way ■

37% | 37% | 26%

Source: *From Awareness to Funding*, OCLC, 2008

- **There is a lot that people don't know about their public libraries.** People are generally unaware of many of the services provided by their local libraries. They indicate awareness of traditional offerings: books, newspapers, magazines, videos/DVDs, etc., as well as services that provide public access computing and Internet access. However, they have much lower awareness of many of the value-added, community-focused programs, such as programming for seniors and teens, literacy training and book discussion groups. This lack of awareness may not be a deterrent for funding support. Unfamiliarity with the full range of library services does not dampen the positive attitudes about library funding held by Probable Supporters and Super Supporters.

Awareness of services provided by the local public library

Total respondents

Respondents were asked: Below are some services or types of information that public libraries may or may not offer. For each one, please indicate whether or not your local public library offers this.

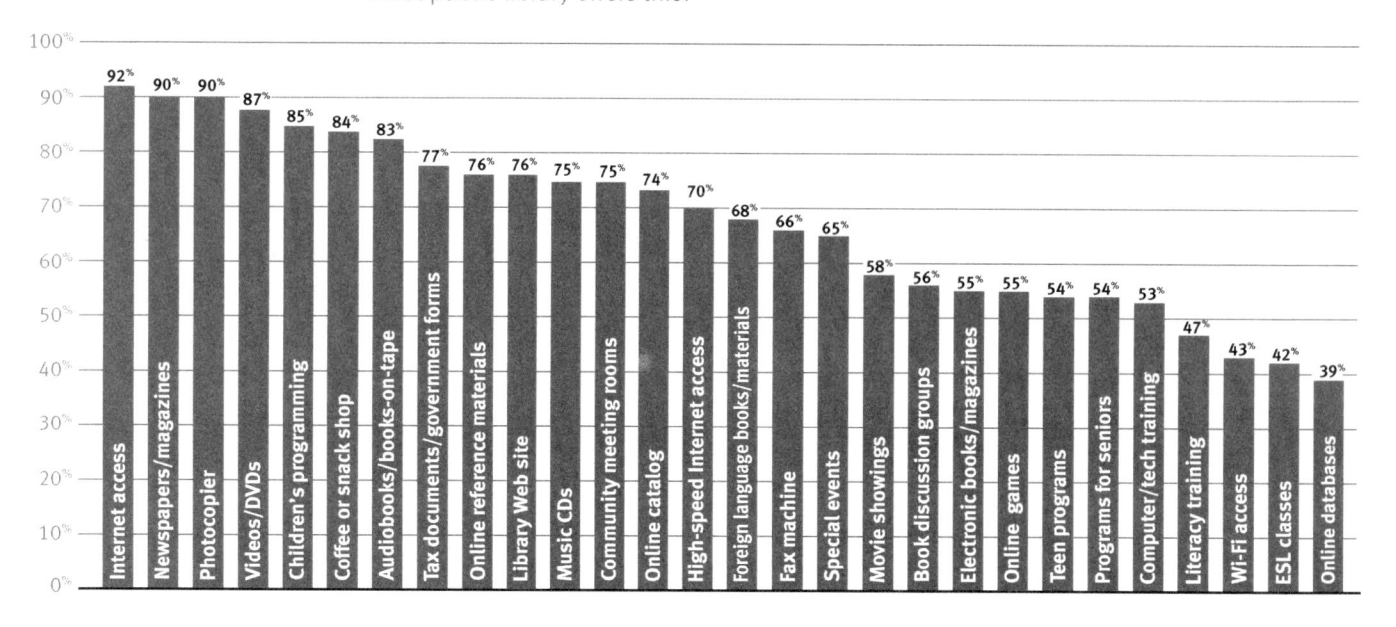

Service	%
Internet access	92%
Newspapers/magazines	90%
Photocopier	90%
Videos/DVDs	87%
Children's programming	85%
Coffee or snack shop	84%
Audiobooks/books-on-tape	83%
Tax documents/government forms	77%
Online reference materials	76%
Library Web site	76%
Music CDs	75%
Community meeting rooms	75%
Online catalog	74%
High-speed Internet access	70%
Foreign language books/materials	68%
Fax machine	66%
Special events	65%
Movie showings	58%
Book discussion groups	56%
Electronic books/magazines	55%
Online games	55%
Teen programs	54%
Programs for seniors	54%
Computer/tech training	53%
Literacy training	47%
Wi-Fi access	43%
ESL classes	42%
Online databases	39%

Percentage of total respondents who said their local public library offered the service.
Source: *From Awareness to Funding*, OCLC, 2008

- **Library support is only marginally related to visitation**. Advocating for library support to library users focuses effort and energy on the wrong target group. In fact, the research showed that frequency of library visitation has almost no relationship to a person's willingness to support the library at the ballot box. Super Supporters show the greatest commitment to library funding support—almost three times the average—yet their frequency of library visits is only slightly above average. And the Just for Fun segment are the heaviest users of the library, but the least likely of the Probable Supporters to definitely vote to fund the library.

Library visitation and *definite* library support by segment

Total voting respondents

Respondents were asked: How many times have you visited your local public library in the past 12 months? If there was a referendum, ballot initiative or bond measure for your local public library on the ballot, how do you think you would vote?

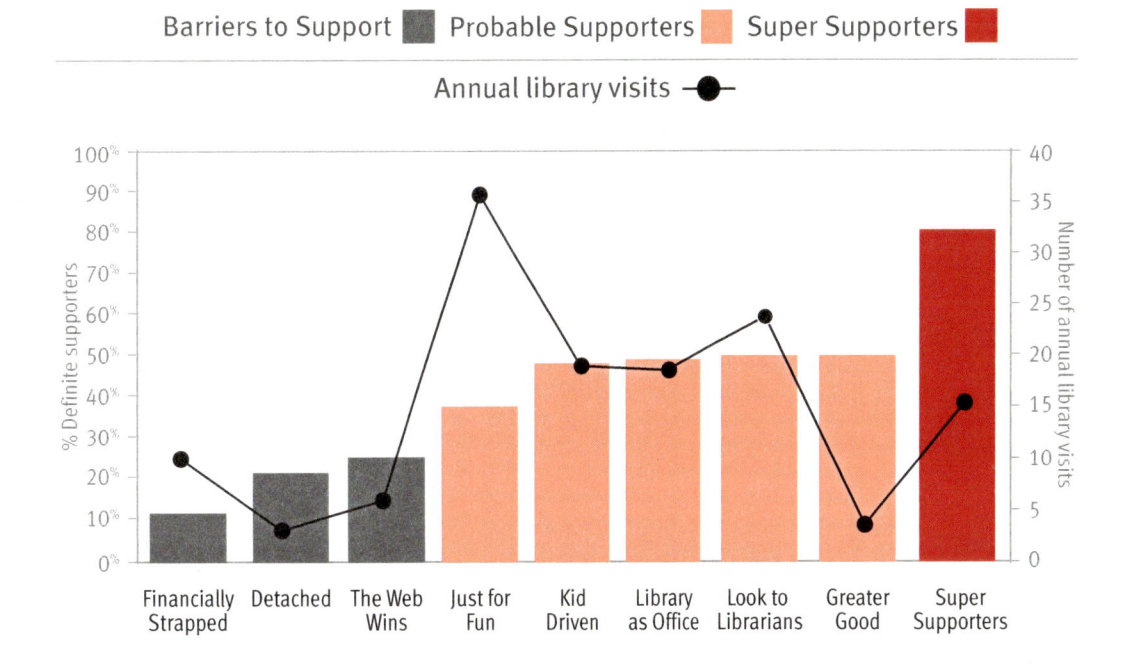

Barriers to Support ■ Probable Supporters ■ Super Supporters ■

Annual library visits ●

Percentage of total voting respondents who would *definitely* vote 'yes' for a library referendum.
Source: *From Awareness to Funding*, OCLC, 2008

- **Perceptions of the librarian are highly related to support.** Passionate librarians who are involved in the community make a difference. Survey respondents rated the librarians at their local public libraries across a number of attributes. Analysis of the responses shows that a strong positive rating for the librarian across five of these attributes has a strong influence on library funding support. Attributes of the 'Passionate Librarian' are:

  - True advocate for lifelong learning
  - Passionate about keeping the library relevant
  - Knowledgeable about every aspect of the library
  - Well-educated
  - Knowledgeable about their community.

The 'Passionate Librarian' and *definite* library support

Total voting respondents

Respondents were asked: Please rate the librarians at the public library in your community on the following traits using a 10-point scale, where a 10 means 'Describes them extremely well' and a 1 means 'Doesn't describe them at all.'

If there was a referendum, ballot initiative or bond measure for your local public library on the ballot, how do you think you would vote?

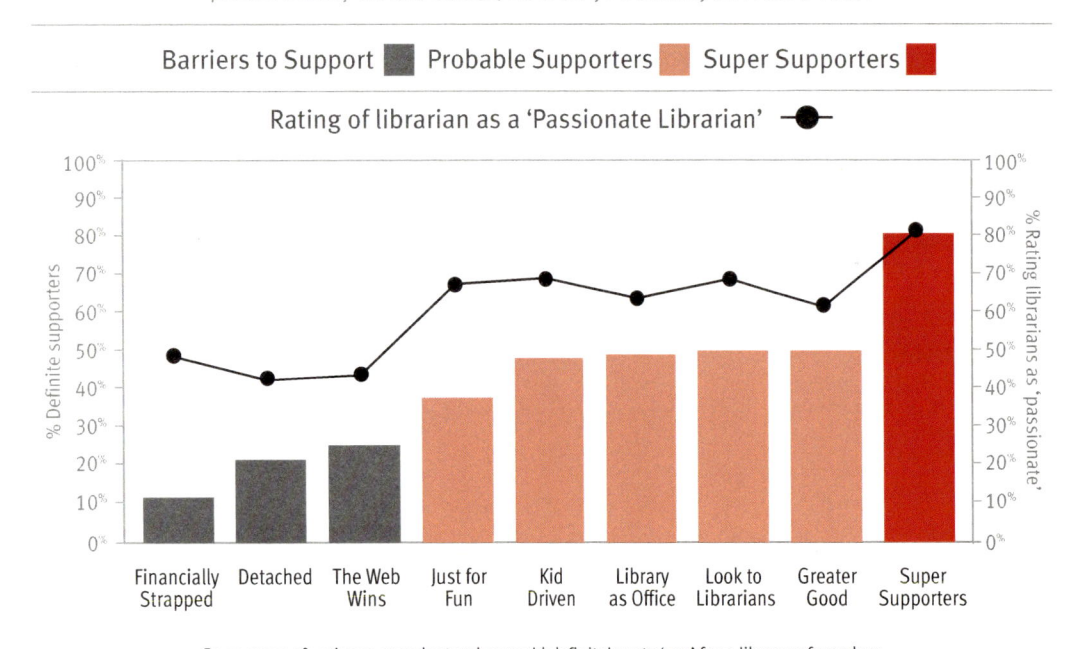

Legend: Barriers to Support ■ Probable Supporters ■ Super Supporters ■
Rating of librarian as a 'Passionate Librarian' ●

[Chart showing % Definite supporters and % Rating librarians as 'passionate' across categories: Financially Strapped, Detached, The Web Wins, Just for Fun, Kid Driven, Library as Office, Look to Librarians, Greater Good, Super Supporters]

Percentage of voting respondents who would definitely vote 'yes' for a library referendum.
Percentage of voting respondents who rated their librarian as a 'Passionate Librarian' with an agreement rating of 8, 9 or 10.
Source: *From Awareness to Funding*, OCLC, 2008

- **The library occupies a very clear position in people's minds as a provider of practical answers and information.** The public library's strong associations as a place for information may not only limit the library's ability to gain mindshare and market share with information seekers, but the current positioning may also be one of the factors hampering the success of library funding initiatives. People's perceptions about the library's ability to transform lives, rather than its role as an information provider, is what drives financial support.

Emotional and intellectual rewards for the public library

Total voting respondents

Respondents were asked: Please rate how well the words or phrases describe the selected brands/categories/activities using a 10-point scale, where a 10 means 'Describes it very well' and a 1 means 'Doesn't describe it at all.'

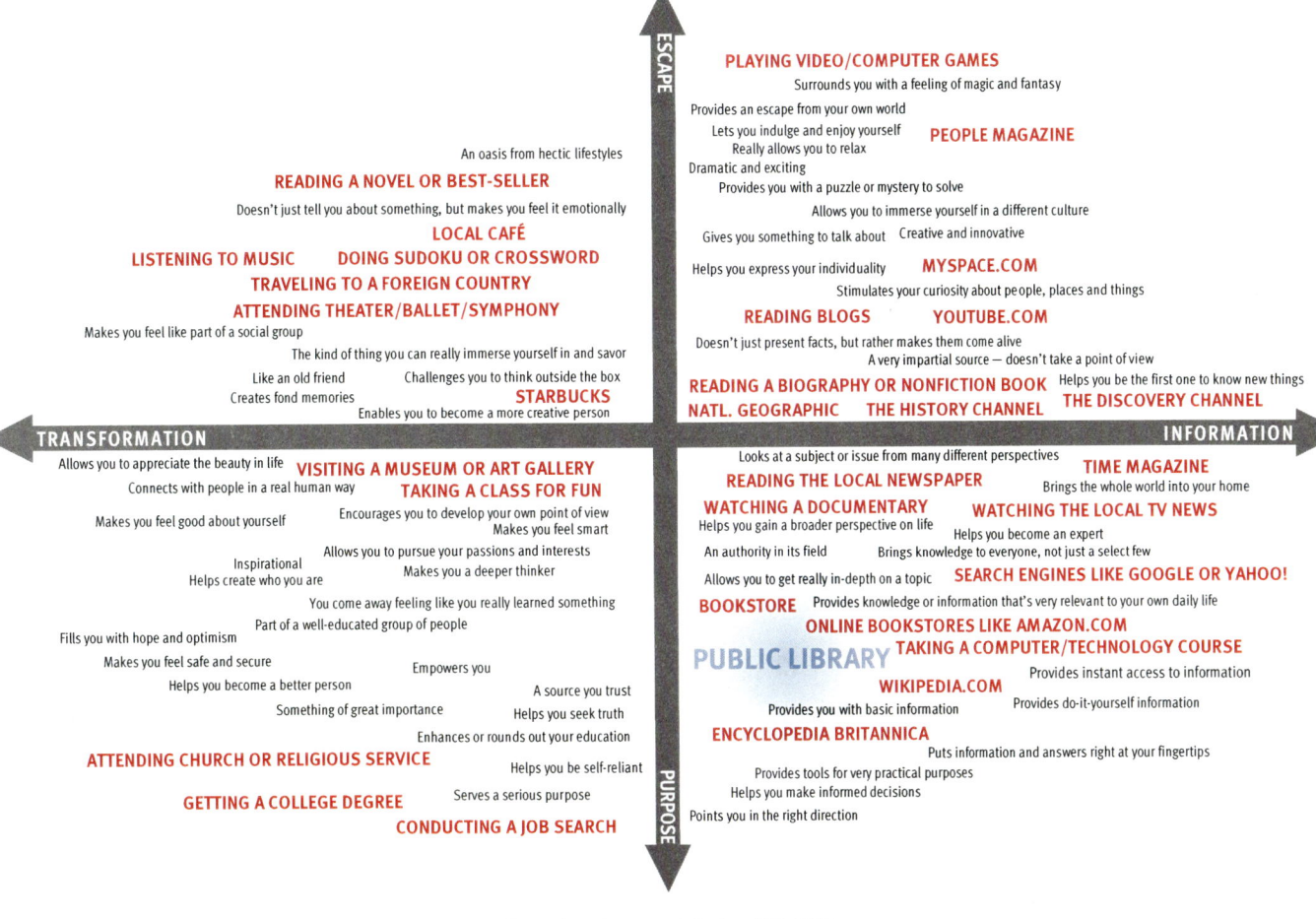

(Four-quadrant chart with axes: ESCAPE (top) / PURPOSE (bottom), TRANSFORMATION (left) / INFORMATION (right))

ESCAPE / TRANSFORMATION quadrant:
- An oasis from hectic lifestyles
- READING A NOVEL OR BEST-SELLER
- Doesn't just tell you about something, but makes you feel it emotionally
- LOCAL CAFÉ
- LISTENING TO MUSIC — DOING SUDOKU OR CROSSWORD
- TRAVELING TO A FOREIGN COUNTRY
- ATTENDING THEATER/BALLET/SYMPHONY
- Makes you feel like part of a social group
- The kind of thing you can really immerse yourself in and savor
- Like an old friend — Challenges you to think outside the box
- Creates fond memories — STARBUCKS
- Enables you to become a more creative person

ESCAPE / INFORMATION quadrant:
- PLAYING VIDEO/COMPUTER GAMES
- Surrounds you with a feeling of magic and fantasy
- Provides an escape from your own world
- Lets you indulge and enjoy yourself — PEOPLE MAGAZINE
- Really allows you to relax
- Dramatic and exciting
- Provides you with a puzzle or mystery to solve
- Allows you to immerse yourself in a different culture
- Gives you something to talk about — Creative and innovative
- Helps you express your individuality — MYSPACE.COM
- Stimulates your curiosity about people, places and things
- READING BLOGS — YOUTUBE.COM
- Doesn't just present facts, but rather makes them come alive
- A very impartial source — doesn't take a point of view
- READING A BIOGRAPHY OR NONFICTION BOOK — Helps you be the first one to know new things
- NATL. GEOGRAPHIC — THE HISTORY CHANNEL — THE DISCOVERY CHANNEL

PURPOSE / TRANSFORMATION quadrant:
- Allows you to appreciate the beauty in life
- VISITING A MUSEUM OR ART GALLERY
- Connects with people in a real human way
- TAKING A CLASS FOR FUN
- Encourages you to develop your own point of view
- Makes you feel good about yourself — Makes you feel smart
- Allows you to pursue your passions and interests
- Inspirational — Makes you a deeper thinker
- Helps create who you are
- You come away feeling like you really learned something
- Fills you with hope and optimism — Part of a well-educated group of people
- Makes you feel safe and secure — Empowers you
- Helps you become a better person — A source you trust
- Something of great importance — Helps you seek truth
- Enhances or rounds out your education
- ATTENDING CHURCH OR RELIGIOUS SERVICE
- Helps you be self-reliant
- GETTING A COLLEGE DEGREE — Serves a serious purpose
- CONDUCTING A JOB SEARCH

PURPOSE / INFORMATION quadrant:
- Looks at a subject or issue from many different perspectives
- READING THE LOCAL NEWSPAPER — TIME MAGAZINE
- Brings the whole world into your home
- WATCHING A DOCUMENTARY — WATCHING THE LOCAL TV NEWS
- Helps you gain a broader perspective on life
- Helps you become an expert
- An authority in its field — Brings knowledge to everyone, not just a select few
- Allows you to get really in-depth on a topic
- SEARCH ENGINES LIKE GOOGLE OR YAHOO!
- BOOKSTORE — Provides knowledge or information that's very relevant to your own daily life
- ONLINE BOOKSTORES LIKE AMAZON.COM
- **PUBLIC LIBRARY** — TAKING A COMPUTER/TECHNOLOGY COURSE
- Provides instant access to information
- WIKIPEDIA.COM
- Provides you with basic information — Provides do-it-yourself information
- ENCYCLOPEDIA BRITANNICA
- Puts information and answers right at your fingertips
- Provides tools for very practical purposes
- Helps you make informed decisions
- Points you in the right direction

Source: *From Awareness to Funding*, OCLC, 2008

- **Belief that the library is a transformational force in people's lives is directly related to their level of funding support.** Aggregation of results across all survey respondents indicates that the public library is viewed as a service that provides the emotional and intellectual rewards of 'purposeful information.' But a review of results of those voters who said they would definitely vote in favor of a library referendum provides a very important distinction. The degree to which the public library was perceived as transformational is significantly higher among the most committed funding supporters (voters who said they would definitely vote yes for a library referendum, ballot initiative or bond measure).

Perceptions of the public library held by people who will definitely vote in support of library funding

Respondents who would definitely vote yes for a library referendum

Respondents were asked: Please rate how well the words or phrases describe the selected brands/categories/activities using a 10-point scale, where a 10 means 'Describes it very well' and a 1 means 'Doesn't describe it at all.'

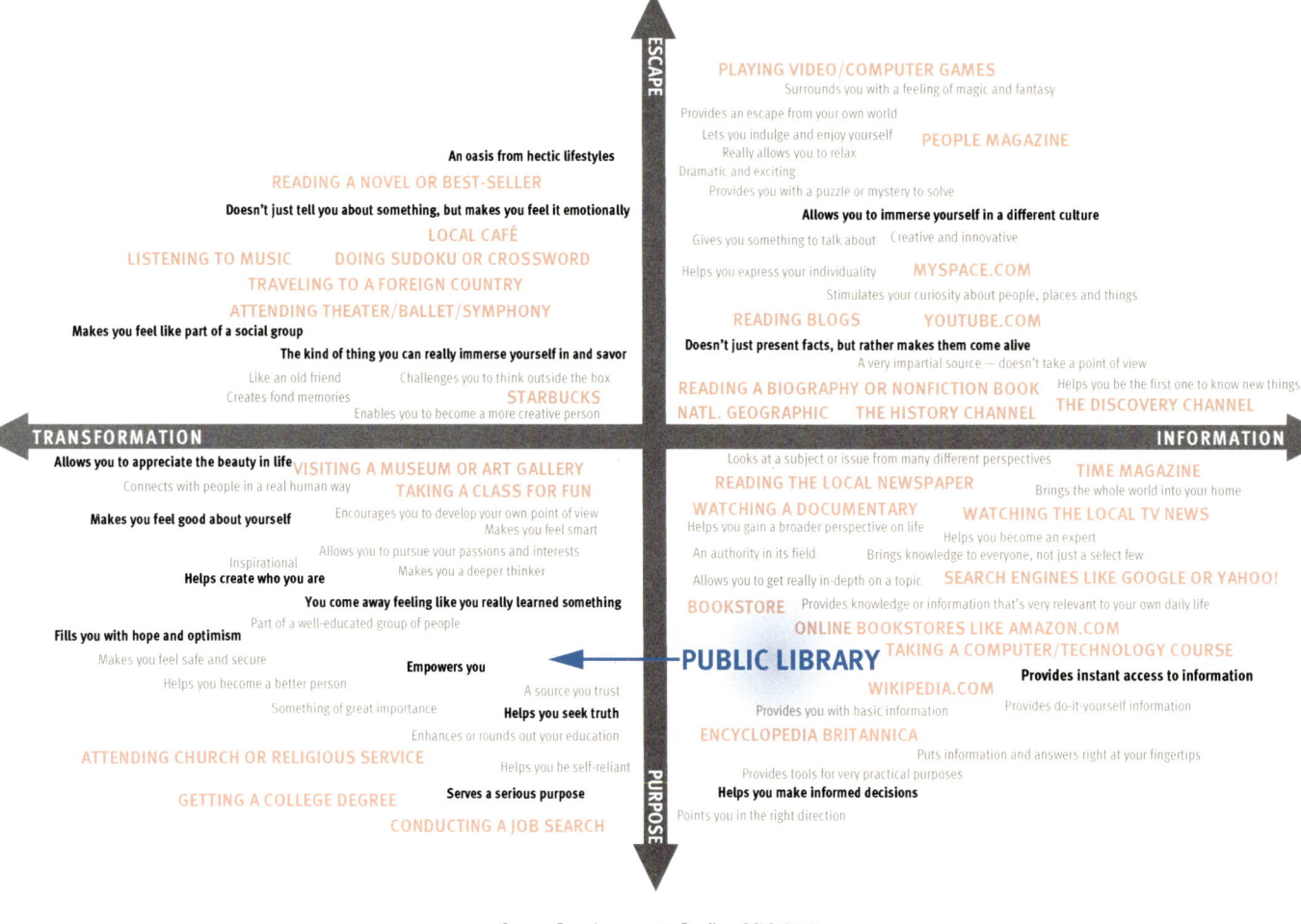

Axes: ESCAPE (up) / PURPOSE (down); TRANSFORMATION (left) / INFORMATION (right)

ESCAPE quadrant — upper right (INFORMATION side):
- PLAYING VIDEO/COMPUTER GAMES — Surrounds you with a feeling of magic and fantasy
- Provides an escape from your own world
- Lets you indulge and enjoy yourself
- Really allows you to relax
- PEOPLE MAGAZINE
- Dramatic and exciting
- Provides you with a puzzle or mystery to solve
- Allows you to immerse yourself in a different culture
- Gives you something to talk about — Creative and innovative
- Helps you express your individuality — MYSPACE.COM
- Stimulates your curiosity about people, places and things
- READING BLOGS — YOUTUBE.COM
- Doesn't just present facts, but rather makes them come alive
- A very impartial source — doesn't take a point of view
- READING A BIOGRAPHY OR NONFICTION BOOK — Helps you be the first one to know new things
- NATL. GEOGRAPHIC — THE HISTORY CHANNEL — THE DISCOVERY CHANNEL

ESCAPE quadrant — upper left (TRANSFORMATION side):
- An oasis from hectic lifestyles
- READING A NOVEL OR BEST-SELLER
- Doesn't just tell you about something, but makes you feel it emotionally
- LOCAL CAFÉ
- LISTENING TO MUSIC — DOING SUDOKU OR CROSSWORD
- TRAVELING TO A FOREIGN COUNTRY
- ATTENDING THEATER/BALLET/SYMPHONY
- Makes you feel like part of a social group
- The kind of thing you can really immerse yourself in and savor
- Like an old friend — Challenges you to think outside the box
- Creates fond memories — STARBUCKS
- Enables you to become a more creative person

PURPOSE quadrant — lower left (TRANSFORMATION side):
- Allows you to appreciate the beauty in life
- VISITING A MUSEUM OR ART GALLERY
- Connects with people in a real human way — TAKING A CLASS FOR FUN
- Makes you feel good about yourself — Encourages you to develop your own point of view
- Makes you feel smart
- Allows you to pursue your passions and interests
- Inspirational — Makes you a deeper thinker
- Helps create who you are
- You come away feeling like you really learned something
- Part of a well-educated group of people
- Fills you with hope and optimism
- Makes you feel safe and secure
- Empowers you ← **PUBLIC LIBRARY**
- Helps you become a better person — A source you trust
- Something of great importance — Helps you seek truth
- Enhances or rounds out your education
- ATTENDING CHURCH OR RELIGIOUS SERVICE — Helps you be self-reliant
- GETTING A COLLEGE DEGREE — Serves a serious purpose
- CONDUCTING A JOB SEARCH

PURPOSE quadrant — lower right (INFORMATION side):
- Looks at a subject or issue from many different perspectives
- READING THE LOCAL NEWSPAPER — TIME MAGAZINE
- WATCHING A DOCUMENTARY — Brings the whole world into your home
- Helps you gain a broader perspective on life — WATCHING THE LOCAL TV NEWS
- An authority in its field — Helps you become an expert
- Allows you to get really in-depth on a topic — Brings knowledge to everyone, not just a select few
- SEARCH ENGINES LIKE GOOGLE OR YAHOO!
- BOOKSTORE — Provides knowledge or information that's very relevant to your own daily life
- ONLINE BOOKSTORES LIKE AMAZON.COM
- TAKING A COMPUTER/TECHNOLOGY COURSE
- Provides instant access to information
- WIKIPEDIA.COM
- Provides you with basic information — Provides do-it-yourself information
- ENCYCLOPEDIA BRITANNICA
- Puts information and answers right at your fingertips
- Provides tools for very practical purposes
- Helps you make informed decisions
- Points you in the right direction

Source: *From Awareness to Funding*, OCLC, 2008

- **Increasing support for libraries may not necessarily mean a trade-off of financial support for other public services**. Increasing funding support for libraries in the Super Supporter and Probable Supporter segments does not necessarily lead to a decrease in support for other locally funded public services. In fact, placing the library in the consideration set with other key local services can increase the level of awareness and importance of the interrelationship with other local services.

A side-by-side comparison of the willingness of a voter segment to increase taxes to fund local public services, including the public library, shows that a willingness to fund one service is often similar to their willingness to support other local services. For example, the most committed library funding supporters, Super Supporters, show a strong intent to vote yes in support of library referendum: 83 percent agreed strongly that they would be willing to raise their taxes to fund the public library. Community support from Super Supporters does not just include support for the public library. In fact, Super Supporters of libraries are also 'super' in their financial support of other locally funded public services.

Over half of all Super Supporters indicated they would support a tax increase for each of the public services surveyed

Super Supporters

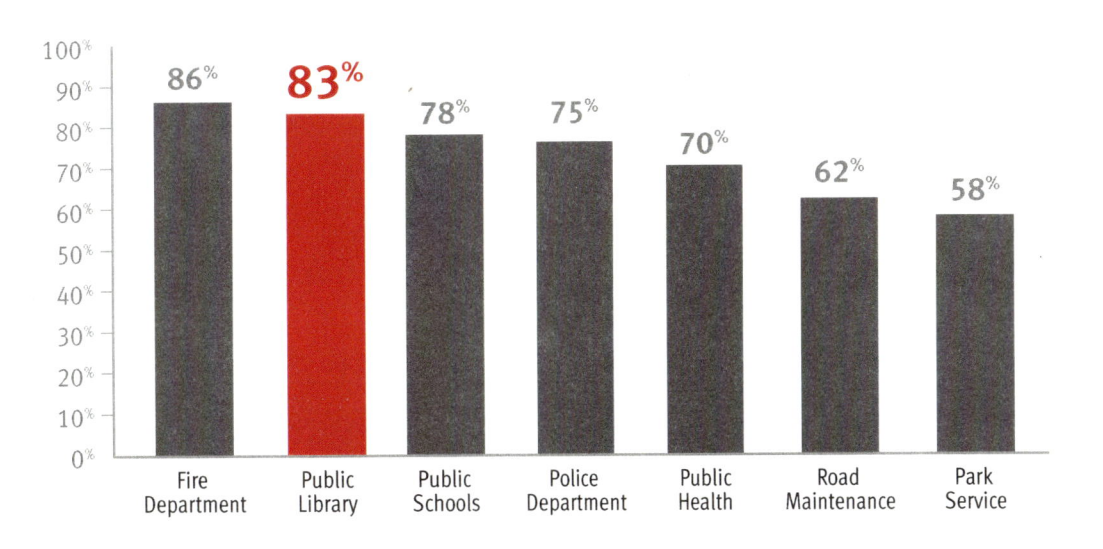

Service	Percentage
Fire Department	86%
Public Library	83%
Public Schools	78%
Police Department	75%
Public Health	70%
Road Maintenance	62%
Park Service	58%

Percentage of Super Supporters who indicated they would support a tax increase for each of the public services surveyed. Source: *From Awareness to Funding*, OCLC, 2008

- **Elected officials support the library—but are not fully committed to increasing funding.** Elected officials are similar to Probable Supporters in their overall attitudes about public library support and funding. However, positive associations do not necessarily translate into support for funding increases.

At the time of the survey, the majority of surveyed elected officials (74 percent) indicated their libraries had enough day-to-day operating funds. The library is often not a top priority for elected officials; they are managing a long list of important public services that are in need of financial support and many face increasing pressure by their constituencies to limit local tax increases.

The library places in the bottom half of the list of public services that elected officials are willing to support with a tax increase

Elected officials

Respondents were asked: For each service, please rate how much you agree with the phrase "I'd be willing to pay more in local taxes to better fund this service." Please use a 10-point scale, where a 10 means you 'Completely Agree' and a 1 means you 'Completely Disagree.'

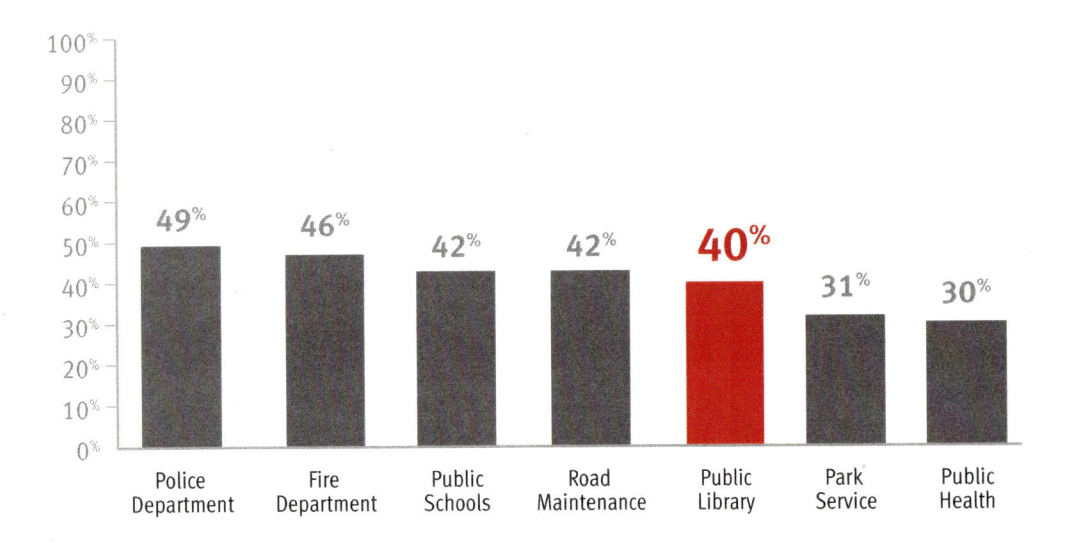

Service	Percentage
Police Department	49%
Fire Department	46%
Public Schools	42%
Road Maintenance	42%
Public Library	40%
Park Service	31%
Public Health	30%

Percentage of elected officials with an agreement rating of 8, 9 or 10.
Source: *From Awareness to Funding*, OCLC, 2008

Understanding supporter attitudes

Qualitative research provided more context about the attitudes, perceptions and beliefs about libraries, librarians and library funding of the two main market segments: Probable Supporters and Super Supporters. While both groups hold many similar attitudes, a comparison of these two groups highlighted a difference in intensity in their emotional connection to the library and their commitment to library support.

Super Supporters are more likely to view the library as holding a transformational role in the community and less likely to question the need to provide ongoing support. Super Supporters are also proactive in articulating their support. Probable Supporters share the belief that the library can change lives and see the library's role in bringing the community together, but are more likely to see the library's role in practical, less transformational terms.

Focus groups showed that even the most avid library supporters have concerns about the relevance of the public library in today's world, and their favorable vote in support of funding initiatives cannot be assumed. While Probable Supporters and Super Supporters have a strong emotional connection to the public library, that connection is latent and is exhibited only when asked directly. The research indicated several barriers that any library support marketing campaign would need to overcome, including the lack of awareness of how local public libraries are funded.

The positive emotional connections that Probable Supporters and Super Supporters have with libraries are not always sufficient to convince them to increase library funding. The research indicated a need to appeal to both the heart and mind of the potential voter, positioning the library as an important part of the community's infrastructure that plays a key role in providing equal access to resources vital for thriving in today's digital world. To make the case for funding and to have long-term impact on local funding for public libraries, a successful campaign would have to change common public perceptions about the library, and its value to individuals and the community.

The library must be repositioned as a vital part of the community infrastructure—now and in the future—that provides transformational opportunities, and a tangible return on investment for individuals and the community as a whole.

The library needs to be positioned as a vital part of the community infrastructure

The library must be repositioned. The library can no longer be viewed as an historical institution that is 'nice to have,' but rather as a vital part of the community infrastructure.

From	To
Information	My transformation
Institution	Infrastructure
Nice to have	Necessity
Past	My future
Altruism for others	ROI for me

Information: The library is one of many sources of information. It could potentially be replaced by a combination of bookstores, schools, coffee shops and the Internet.

Transformation: The library is not about 'information,' it is about 'transformation,' for people and my community.

Institution: The library is an institution sometimes associated with an out-of-date building, aged materials and limited accessibility. (The library has limited hours, the Internet is available 24/7.)

Infrastructure: The library is not an outdated institution. It is a vital part of community infrastructure.

Nice to have: Availability of so many other options for information and learning make the library a 'nice to have' service, rather than a necessity.

Necessity: The library is not simply a 'nice to have' service—it is a necessity. It provides equal access to technology, helping bridge the digital divide.

Past: The library is an important part of supporters' lives, but they question whether it is still relevant for their children and grandchildren.

Future: The library is not a nostalgic building or set of programs. The library provides services and infrastructure for the future.

Altruism for others: The library is less important to them, but it is important for 'other people' in the community.

Return on investment: Library funding support is not based only on a vague sense of altruism, but based on a real economic return for individuals, families and communities.

Summary

The research made clear that an effective library advocacy and marketing campaign in support of increased library funding must ensure that the library is repositioned as both a unique and essential part of the community infrastructure. It must attract attention and have stopping power. The library cannot be viewed as a place of information that's 'nice to have,' but as a 'must have' that's as important to the future as the past. An effective campaign must present today's library as a place of possibilities and as a critical asset—for individuals (to find jobs, reeducate themselves and enhance literacy) and for the community (access to technology, continued education and economic benefits).

Geek the Library: A Pilot

Chapter 2

We geek creativity

Geek the Library, a community-based public awareness campaign, was piloted between June 2009 and April 2010. The campaign is bold and simple, and focuses on the critical role that public libraries play in our communities while raising awareness of local library funding challenges.

The campaign uses a multipronged approach and includes three distinct steps: raising awareness, changing attitudes/perceptions and driving behavior/intended behavior. This chapter covers campaign goals and objectives, target audiences, the concept and approach, and the pilot libraries.

Ambitious goals and clear objectives

The goal of the Geek the Library project was to design, execute, measure and disseminate a public awareness campaign that uses advocacy and marketing to increase awareness of the vital role public libraries play and library funding challenges.

The pilot campaign, conducted between June 2009 and April 2010, needed to effectively change a variety of library and library funding perceptions held by Probable Supporters and Super Supporters.

- **Shift public perceptions about the library.** Communicate to the public that the library is relevant and vital—to individuals and the community. Not only can people explore their passions—whatever those might be—but they can apply for a job or investigate opportunities that could change their lives.

- **Bring new light to people's perceptions of librarians.** Remind the public about the passionate librarians who are: true advocates for lifelong learning, enthusiastic about making the library relevant, knowledgeable about every aspect of the library, well-educated and knowledgeable about the community.

- **Elevate the library as a valuable community asset.** Educate the public that many studies support the idea that dollars spent on libraries provide solid economic returns to the community.

- **Position the library as transformational.** Explain to the public that libraries give people hope. They can find new opportunities, reeducate themselves, realize their dreams and transform their lives—every day—regardless of economic standing.

- **Awaken latent support.** Educate the public that library funding is not keeping up with demand and that the bulk of library funding is from the local purse. Remind them that they have a role in supporting their library.

The campaign also needed to stand out from the large number of marketing and advertising messages targeted at U.S. consumers on a daily basis. It needed to make the library personally relevant to potential supporters, raise awareness, drive action and spark conversation—all while adhering to guidelines that restrict lobbying by libraries. In addition, the campaign had to increase library support in local communities by educating and motivating Probable Supporters and mobilizing Super Supporters.

Campaign target audiences

From Awareness to Funding: A study of library support in America identified two key tiers of library funding supporters: Super Supporters and Probable Supporters. These supporter segments, along with influential members of the community, such as local officials, are important target audiences for an effective public awareness campaign.

The research indicates that targeting these groups and using a message specifically designed to move them, has the potential to improve awareness of library funding needs and impact library perceptions to enhance library support.

Super Supporters

Super Supporters represent the public library's core supporter group and play an important role in helping to bring the campaign out into the community.

A Super Supporter:

- Believes the library is a place where people can better themselves
- Recognizes the library's contribution to a successful community
- Is well-known, well-informed, influential and not afraid to openly voice opinions
- Is likely to vote in both general and local elections
- Almost always votes in favor of library referendums.

Probable Supporters

Probable Supporters, the main target audience for the campaign, support the library, but their favorable vote is not a given.

A Probable Supporter:

- Does not frequently visit the library, but appreciates the library's overall contribution to the community
- Recognizes that the research/information the library provides is superior to the Internet
- Believes the library is a key partner in a child's education
- Does not oppose raising taxes to fund the public library.

Influential members of the community

This group, also considered a target audience for the campaign, comprises well-respected individuals who are part of the community's leadership and often speak out about important local issues.

Examples:

- Elected and appointed officials
- Local business owners or leaders
- Local celebrities, such as local radio and TV on-air personalities
- Magazine/newspaper editors
- Consumer advocacy organization representatives
- School administrators and teachers
- Simply someone whose opinion many community members trust.

Concept and approach

Geek the Library was developed as a library support brand that provides the tools to help public libraries position themselves as personally relevant to individuals and vital to the community. The aim was to measure the campaign's potential to help reverse the downward funding trend in the U.S.

The campaign idea, Geek the Library, was evaluated through focus groups with Probable Supporters and Super Supporters. The campaign concept was also tested with a number of public library directors. Input from these focus groups was used as guidance to finalize the concept and material development.

> **Geek/Verb**
> 1: To love, to enjoy, to celebrate, to have an intense passion for
> 2: To express interest in
> 3: To possess a large amount of knowledge
> 4: To promote

These days, "geek" doesn't necessarily mean a nerdy kid with glasses. In fact, contemporary use of the term geek is hip and often positive. Being a geek, or being passionate about a topic or activity, is something to be admired. Changing the noun "geek" to a verb created a new approach to promoting the value of the library for individuals and the community—and educating the public about library funding.

Using a language and visual approach that was unexpected from the library and one that made people think about what they "geek" helped break through the marketing clutter and got people talking. Feedback from pilot libraries confirmed that the concept, while simple, has the potential to make considerable impact. The campaign's core message—everyone has something they are passionate about, something they geek and the library supports it all—resonated with a large percentage of residents in pilot communities.

Photographs of individuals and the things that they "geek" provide the core of the campaign and are woven into Geek the Library materials, including ads, banners, the Web site and grassroots programs. The featured individuals represent a cross-section of demographics, genders and ethnicities—reinforcing the fact that the library is for everyone.

I geek barbecue	I geek beekeeping	I geek composting
I geek engineering	I geek football	I geek hiphop
I geek schooners	I geek silentfilms	I geek superheroes
I geek vampires	I geek worms	I geek art

Geek the Library: A Community Awareness Campaign

Pilot libraries

Testing the campaign in the field was critical and we cannot thank the pilot participants enough for their passion, creativity and perseverance. Pilot participants were selected based on a variety of criteria including: funding need, library funding structure, U.S. geographic location, and willingness and capacity of state and local library partners. Most importantly, the pilot markets needed to be representative of a large proportion of U.S. public libraries. Two regions were selected, southern Georgia and central Iowa, to launch the awareness campaign in June 2009. Pilot libraries and systems were selected as pilot locations based on several factors including: strong library leadership, mix of urban and rural libraries, structure and level of local funding, and willingness to test new ideas.

Pilot participants in Georgia included libraries from Live Oak Public Libraries, Ohoopee Regional Library System, Okefenokee Regional Library System, Satilla Regional Library, Screven-Jenkins Regional Library, Statesboro Regional Library System and Three Rivers Regional Library System. Pilot participants in Iowa included the Des Moines Public Library and Ames Public Library, and other libraries in Dallas, Polk, Story and Warren Counties. (A full list of pilot libraries can be found in Appendix B.)

A smaller group of pilot participants was added at the end of 2009 representing Piedmont, Georgia; Milwaukee, Wisconsin; Shelbyville, Indiana; and Zion, Illinois. These libraries and library systems received individual grants to support campaign initiatives. These markets were added to test execution of the program with a reduced investment, a smaller amount of direct field support and increased reliance on the library staff to develop the marketing plan, and identify advertising opportunities, events and other campaign activities.

All pilot libraries received support and guidance from the field marketing team, and a supply of campaign materials such as posters, handouts, stickers, bookmarks and bags, and access to digital artwork for use online and on computers in the library.

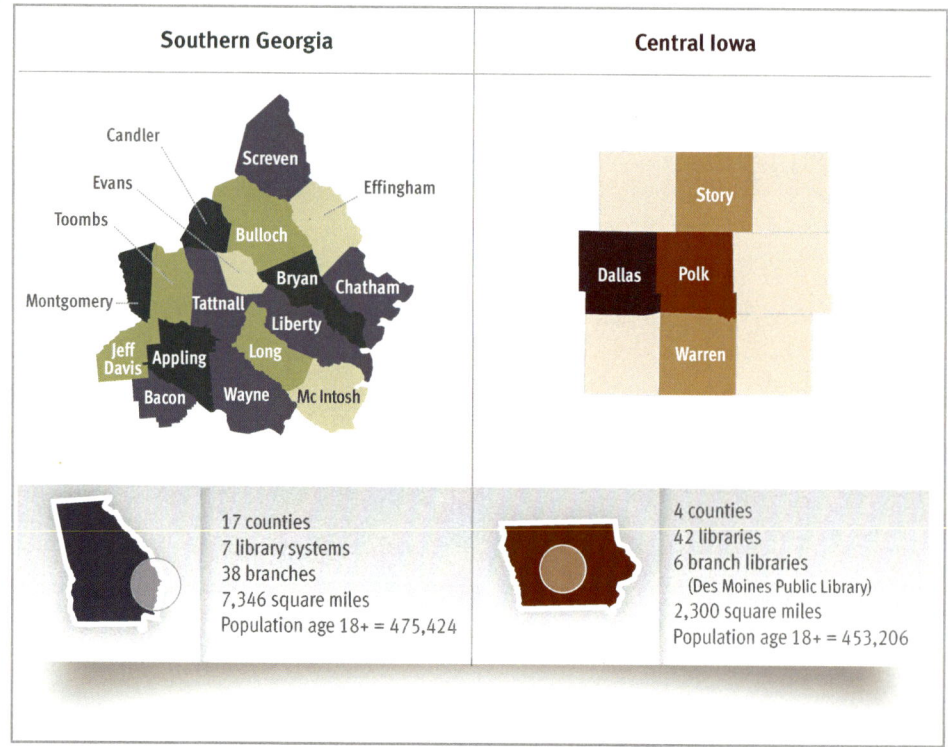

Southern Georgia

Counties: Candler, Screven, Evans, Effingham, Toombs, Bulloch, Bryan, Chatham, Montgomery, Tattnall, Liberty, Jeff Davis, Appling, Long, Bacon, Wayne, McIntosh

17 counties
7 library systems
38 branches
7,346 square miles
Population age 18+ = 475,424

Central Iowa

Counties: Story, Dallas, Polk, Warren

4 counties
42 libraries
6 branch libraries
  (Des Moines Public Library)
2,300 square miles
Population age 18+ = 453,206

2-6 Geek the Library: A Pilot

Elements of the campaign

The Geek the Library pilot campaign was designed as a multipronged marketing approach, incorporating traditional advertising techniques along with promotional efforts, such as events and presentations to local community organizations. The pilot campaign utilized a broad range of marketing and advertising tactics—including e-mail marketing, online marketing, public relations initiatives, grassroots programs and a campaign Web site (geekthelibrary.org). Promotional tactics were spread out over time, proactively and consistently connecting the public to information about the value of the library and its role in the community and public library funding.

I geek worms

The library helps everyone explore the things they geek. With Internet access for all, knowledgeable librarians and local programs, the library is an important resource for your community. Keep your library vital by turning your passions into support. Get your geek on. Show your support.

geekthelibrary.org

Brought to you by OCLC, a nonprofit library cooperative, with funding by a grant from the Bill & Melinda Gates Foundation. Geekthelibrary.org does not support or oppose any candidate for public office and does not take positions on legislation.

Advertising

Advertising played an important role in introducing the campaign and creating a buzz throughout the pilot communities. Advertising formats included newspaper, radio, billboard and online. A consistent and ongoing advertising plan in the first few months—especially newspaper—made community engagement efforts, such as events, much more successful by establishing strong campaign awareness and piquing the public's curiosity.

Community events

Local community events played an integral role in allowing participating library staff to take the campaign out into the community and engage directly with residents.

Participation in local events helped spark interest in the campaign, and it gave pilot library staff and leaders critical opportunities to discuss Geek the Library one-on-one. Some pilot library participants also reported that attending additional and more diverse events helped rejuvenate general public interest about the library.

Geek the Library banners and table skirts were used by many libraries, and a branded kiosk was used for bigger events, such as the Savannah Children's Festival and the Iowa State Fair. Additionally, the Geek the Library field team worked with libraries to develop successful strategies for engaging the public, and helping them make the connection between the campaign, the library and library funding.

Giveaways, including posters, stickers, bumper stickers and bookmarks, were always popular. T-shirts were the ultimate prize and used for raffles and to encourage Web site e-mail sign-ups. Geek walls (free-standing walls that people could write on to share what they geek) provided a simple and fun way for people to connect personally with the campaign.

Telling the story

One of the most widely used campaign elements was the Geek the Library handout. It educated readers by telling the full campaign story, including the main issue that public libraries are struggling and every individual plays a role in library support. This piece was given out at events, in the library and at community presentations, was included in mailings and also was used as a newspaper insert.

What do you geek?

Everyone has something they are passionate about—something they geek. Maybe you geek football or hip hop. Maybe you are passionate about organic gardening, classic movies or volunteering. Or maybe you just geek the weather.

Whatever you geek, serious or fun, the public library supports you.

The public library inspires and empowers. With Internet access, knowledgeable librarians and local programs, it is an important resource for your community. And for millions of Americans, it is their only access to essential resources they need to improve their lives. For many, the library is not a luxury, it is a necessity.

The problem is, public libraries are struggling.

Many libraries are cutting staff, programs and hours, and some are closing their doors forever. And even though usage has increased, funding is not sufficient to meet the need.

So please, share whatever you geek. Share what your library does for you and your community. And spread the word that your public library needs everyone's support.

Get your geek on.
Show your support. | **geekthelibrary.org**

Brought to you by OCLC, a nonprofit library cooperative, with funding by a grant from the Bill & Melinda Gates Foundation. Geekthelibrary.org does not support or oppose any candidate for public office and does not take positions on legislation.

Public relations and media relations

Public relations and media relations were critical for building awareness. Geek the Library was introduced to the media at launch events, through localized press releases and with consistent media story pitching in pilot communities throughout the campaign. Pilot libraries were encouraged to build on their existing relationships with local media by communicating campaign updates and appropriate local story angles to maintain coverage at launch and throughout the campaign. Pilot participants shared the local evolution of the campaign with their media contacts, which translated into many meaningful article placements.

Grassroots and localization efforts

Pilot libraries took to the streets to distribute posters and other educational material to local businesses, schools and community organizations. Presentations were used to introduce the campaign to many key community organizations (e.g., chambers of commerce and Kiwanis chapters) and elements of the campaign were localized to encourage partnerships in helping to promote the campaign. Some pilot libraries developed unique personalized posters featuring influential members of the community, such as school administrators and elected officials. To engage residents, postcards were also used as invitations to events, and used with preprinted, localized messages and distributed at events.

geekthelibrary.org

All Geek the Library marketing materials included the URL: geekthelibrary.org. This public Web site provides an introduction to the awareness campaign, as well as advice about how to start the public library funding conversation locally. The Web site acted as a campaign anchor. It provided an important engagement point for consumers excited to do something right away.

Online traffic was monitored and adjustments were made to improve ease of use. Web site visitors signed up for e-mail communications, which were sent out on a weekly basis. Topics included general updates, information about current public library studies and educational messages about library funding. One of the most popular areas of the site was the 'Get Your Geek On' section where visitors could contribute stories about what they geek and help build the virtual geek wall, download materials, and personalize and purchase Geek the Library items from a virtual store.

An online survey provided an opportunity for visitor engagement and for understanding the level of library support of visitors to the site. The survey was based on a version of the original segmentation questionnaire with just a small number of questions, which categorized people by their level of library support into Super Supporters, Probable Supporters, etc. A short poll was added in December 2009. The purpose of the poll was to provide a simple and fun way for first-time visitors to find out something about library funding.

Videos

Twenty-nine original Geek the Library videos were produced in June 2009—most were filmed in the pilot markets. These 30-second videos depicted real people describing what they geek. The videos helped provide a visual representation of the marketing message and were loaded on YouTube to assist the viral spread of the campaign. Later in the pilot campaign, many libraries negotiated with local public access TV channels to run the videos as advertisements, sometimes at no charge.

Social media

The campaign included pages on popular social networking Web sites. Regular posts were made to Facebook and Twitter. The campaign videos, along with many photographs from events, were posted on YouTube, Flickr and geekthelibrary.org. A photo release sign was posted at most events and individual photo releases were signed when appropriate. As the campaign pilot gained momentum, so did the public's discussions on the ground and on the social networking sites. Pilot libraries also used social media to provide timely updates about the campaign and to engage with library supporters in real-time as discussions unfolded.

Tools for libraries and library leaders

Pilot libraries were given a number of materials specifically for use at the library, such as a large hanging banner designed for outdoor use. Library staff used Geek the Library-themed screensavers on patron computers and created interactive displays. They also connected the Geek the Library theme to transformational resources, such as jobs-related and lifelong learning programs and events.

Tools to help library leaders share the Geek the Library campaign and discuss funding in the community were developed and fine-tuned throughout the pilot campaign. Pilot libraries were integral in driving and informing the creation of these resources. This was particularly important for local presentations and meetings or conversations with influential members of the community. Pilot library leaders and staff conducted impressive outreach efforts; and field managers, who worked with the library teams, reported the resulting positive impact in the local communities.

Reaching potential supporters: Three steps to the campaign

Each stage of the campaign was designed to provide a foundation for the next—moving the public through a process whereby they first gained familiarity with the campaign by seeing the message in multiple venues. Next, they engaged with the campaign in ways that were fun, personalized and unexpected while learning more about libraries and library funding. Finally, they made the connection to how they can support their libraries.

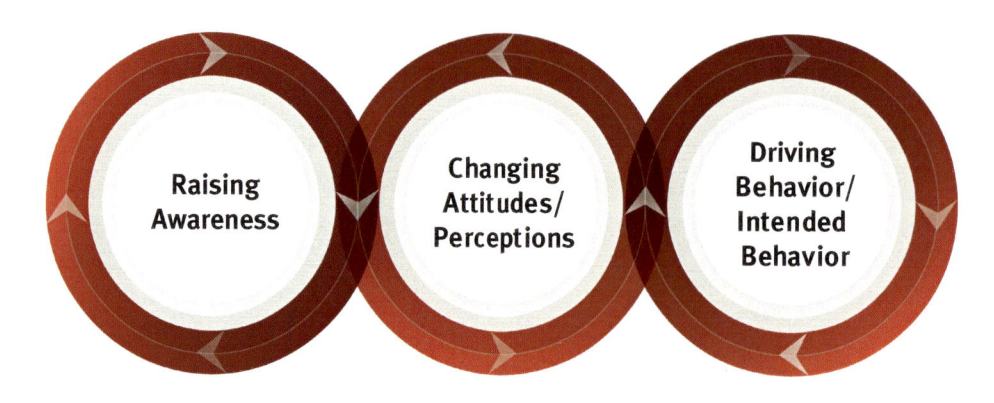

- Raising Awareness
- Changing Attitudes/Perceptions
- Driving Behavior/Intended Behavior

Step 1: Raising Awareness

Advertising and local media exposure was vital to growing campaign awareness in a short time. Consistent advertising initiatives in the first few months, including radio, billboard and newspaper, got residents' attention and created a local buzz in pilot communities. Traditional media outreach (public relations) led to nearly 300 article placements in total, including major newspapers, major network TV affiliates, print, radio and online media in pilot markets. Much of this activity was connected to launch activities and local events, and customized local stories were pitched in pilot markets to generate awareness of funding needs. Leveraging and expanding existing relationships between the libraries and the media was key.

Step 2: Changing Attitudes/Perceptions

Advertising and public relations helped residents begin to think differently about the library. Direct community involvement by library leaders and staff was also a fundamental component of the pilot campaign, helping to inspire and sustain conversations about the growing and important need for increased financial support for public libraries. Pilot libraries accomplished this through presentations and communication with city officials; library supporters and other influential members of the community; in-library promotion and events; partnerships with local businesses, institutions and organizations; and taking part in community events. Residents could also engage online (e.g., sharing their stories) at geekthelibrary.org.

Step 3: Driving Behavior/Intended Behavior

After five months of advertising and exposure at events, the pilot communities had a great deal of campaign awareness and were starting to show some shifts in perception and attitude about the library. Now it was time to make a stronger connection to library funding. The campaign moved to a more serious funding message (I geek my job, I geek transformation, I geek green, I geek my future, I geek community and I geek new ventures) to reinforce the critical transformational services libraries provide. The new materials included six funding-focused print ads and posters, and other materials for libraries to use at Geek the Library events to directly engage the public, particularly influential members of the community such as public officials. Pilot participants were also encouraged to conduct a Geek the Library Week in their communities and they were provided kits to help with public relations efforts during this portion of the campaign.

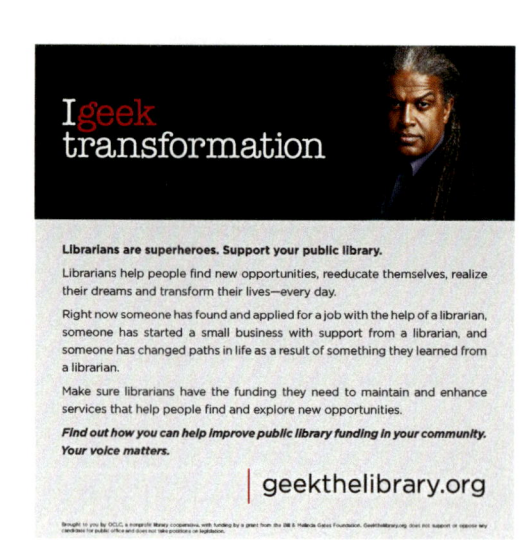

Campaign measurement

Measuring success was an ongoing and multifaceted process. Resident market surveys conducted in southern Georgia and central Iowa prior to launch and after five months in market represent the largest piece of the Geek the Library campaign results. Field managers continuously gathered feedback from participating libraries and used this information to share ideas and improve campaign materials and tools. Ongoing measurement of consumer activity on geekthelibrary.org and social networking sites, plus media mentions, were all used to assemble the most accurate overall assessment of campaign awareness effectiveness.

Summary

Geek the Library is not your typical community awareness campaign. It's bold and personal—and makes a statement. The campaign acts as an overarching platform to get people's attention, help them make a personal connection to the library and to encourage important local library funding conversations. Through all of the campaign elements, such as advertising and community events, participating libraries can effectively raise awareness, change perceptions and drive positive behavior as it relates to library support.

The tireless efforts of the pilot libraries' leaders and staff ensured a complete and successful evaluation of the program in market—a process invaluable to establishing guidelines and best practices for libraries implementing the campaign in the future.

Geek the Library Delivers

Chapter 3

We geek results

Market surveys conducted before and after the pilot campaign, and feedback from participating library leaders and staff, provided evidence that many campaign goals saw positive movement. People noticed it, liked it and took action.

There was unusually strong campaign awareness and campaign familiarity after five months with 49 percent of residents in southern Georgia and 64 percent of residents in central Iowa becoming familiar with the campaign. This chapter shows how Geek the Library helped pilot libraries raise awareness, change public perceptions and drive behavior that could have a positive impact on public library funding—now and in the future.

Measuring impact: Awareness, perceptions and behavior

The Geek the Library pilot campaign was launched in two core markets, southern Georgia and central Iowa, in June 2009. The campaign pilot ran initially through November 2009 and was subsequently extended through April 2010. The impact of the pilot campaign was measured in a number of ways, including direct feedback from participating libraries and ongoing tracking of individual campaign activities, such as Web site traffic, event attendance, press mentions and Facebook activity. Success was determined based on the changes in awareness, perceptions and behavior relating to library support and funding among potential supporters in the pilot communities.

A quantitative survey fielded in June 2009 provided a baseline pre-study of resident awareness, perceptions and library support behavior prior to campaign launch. Changes in those measures following the first five months of the campaign in southern Georgia and central Iowa were captured in a post-study completed in November 2009.

The methodology

The quantitative study targeted 400 respondents in both central Iowa and southern Georgia. The sample in each market included 50 Chronic Non Voters, 50 Barriers to Support and 300 Probable Supporters and Super Supporters, representing the four main segmentation groups identified in the original segmentation study *From Awareness to Funding: A study of library support in America*. Respondents represented U.S. residents between the ages of 18–74. Respondents were interviewed by phone for approximately 20 minutes and, within each market, data were weighted to be representative of age, gender and income.

The baseline pre-campaign survey was fielded June 2–10, 2009 and the post-campaign survey was fielded November 16–28, 2009, excluding Thanksgiving Day. Survey results are referred to as pre- and post-wave in the charts featured in this chapter. Percentages in data tables may not total 100 percent due to rounding or question format. Respondents were sometimes asked to select all responses that may apply or were not required to answer the question.

The goal of the pre- and post-campaign surveys was to evaluate the effectiveness of the Geek the Library Campaign at moving potential supporters through the following stages:

Raising awareness of the campaign and the need for library support.

Changing attitudes and perceptions about the library, the librarian and the need for increased library funding.

Driving behavior that relates to increasing support for the local library.

The Geek the Library pilot had ambitious objectives, a short timeframe and a relatively small financial investment when compared with advertising and marketing campaigns for other commercial brands.

Step one: Raising awareness

The U.S. public is bombarded by thousands of marketing messages a day. The first job of an effective awareness campaign is to cut through the high volume of marketing clutter and be noticed. Before the campaign could change perceptions, it had to reach a significant percentage of residents in the pilot communities, and develop sufficient awareness and interest to make them take notice. Both core markets achieved unusually strong campaign awareness in a five-month window, with 49 percent of residents in southern Georgia and 64 percent of residents in central Iowa becoming familiar with the campaign.

Strong campaign awareness for time in market

Central Iowa and southern Georgia

Respondents were asked: Have you recently seen an ad for the public library featuring a person's face next to wording that says, 'I Geek' followed by a brief description of his or her passion or interest? For example, the ad might say, 'I Geek construction vehicles' or 'I Geek foreign films.' The background of the ad is black. Have you seen an ad for the public library like this?

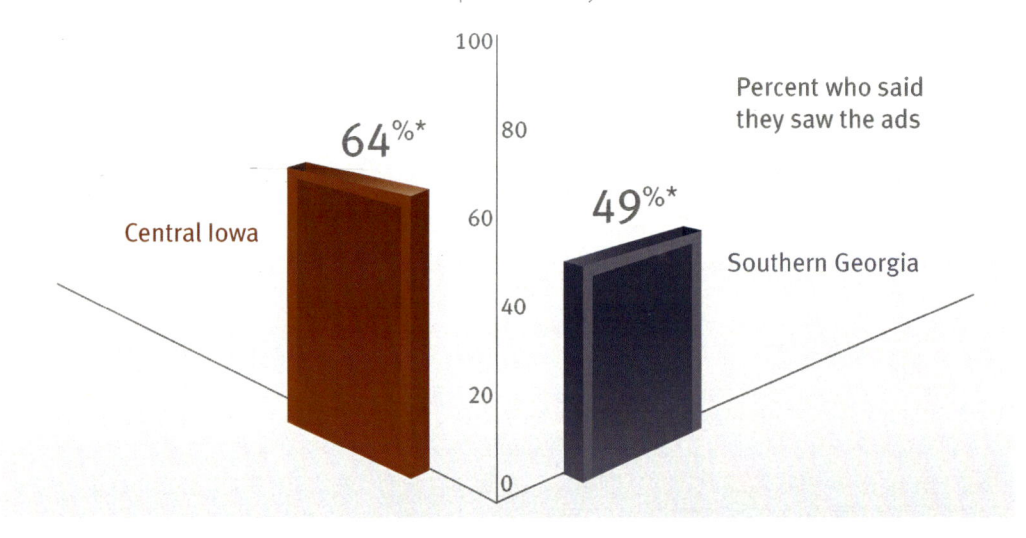

Percent who said they saw the ads

- Central Iowa: 64%*
- Southern Georgia: 49%*

Percentage of respondents who said 'yes.' Asterisks (*) represent ratings significantly higher than the 0.05 level (pre- vs. post-wave).
Source: *Geek the Library: A Community Awareness Campaign*, OCLC, 2011

Many pilot libraries reported that patrons and members of the community noticed the campaign early in the pilot. Residents came into the library specifically to ask about the campaign. At events, residents expressed interest and excitement in the message, saying, "This campaign is everywhere."

Advertising was key to the high levels of campaign awareness. Residents indicated that they had seen the campaign in a wide variety of venues, particularly advertising. There were many similarities in both markets—billboards were most frequently cited as a primary source of where the campaign had been seen. However, it was the combination of the variety of advertising formats and vehicles that was significant to driving awareness. Online ads were more frequently mentioned in southern Georgia, while the campaign got more people's attention at events in central Iowa.

Advertising was a key element in spreading campaign awareness, notably billboards

Central Iowa and southern Georgia

Respondents were asked: In which of the following places have you seen a Geek the Library ad?

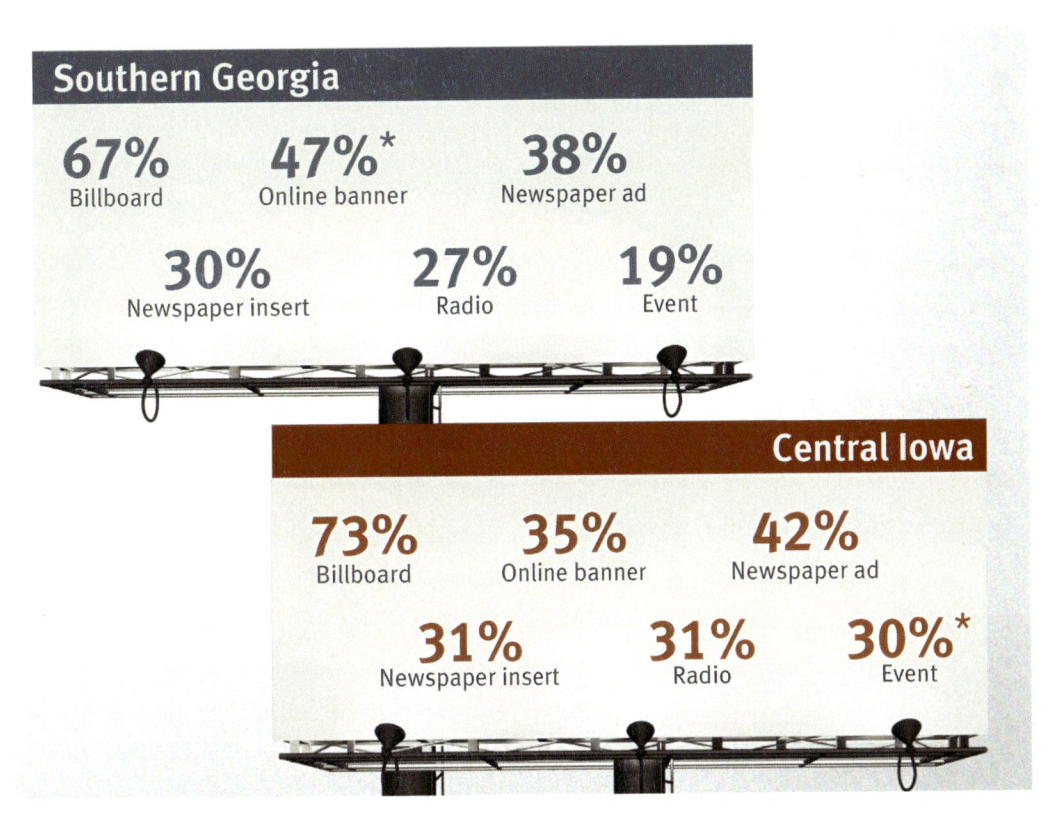

Southern Georgia

67% Billboard	47%* Online banner	38% Newspaper ad
30% Newspaper insert	27% Radio	19% Event

Central Iowa

73% Billboard	35% Online banner	42% Newspaper ad
31% Newspaper insert	31% Radio	30%* Event

Percentage of respondents who saw the ad and saw/heard it at least once in each place.
Asterisks (*) represent ratings significant at the 0.05 level (southern Georgia vs. central Iowa).
Source: *Geek the Library: A Community Awareness Campaign*, OCLC, 2011

One reason the campaign was so successful at generating awareness was its stopping power. It was seen as unique and eye-catching, and unexpected from the public library. Potential supporters also noted that it drew attention to the library.

Do people like the campaign?

Ask most people in your community what they think about the public library and they will likely confirm that they "love" or at least "like" the library and consider it to be a positive influence in the community. When developing Geek the Library, it was important that the campaign idea remain consistent with the universal library brand, and, although the funding situation faced by some public libraries is dire, it was important to avoid negative or threatening messages.

In the marketing and advertising industry, the question, "Do people like the campaign?" is not typically asked—the question is whether the campaign is effective. (Sometimes less likable campaigns have even more impact.) But in this case, we felt there was value in evaluating the campaign's appeal.

The survey asked pilot community residents to rate the campaign's likability. The results show the campaign's appeal to potential supporters. The majority of people in both regions rated the campaign as positive or neutral.

High ratings for likability in both markets
Central Iowa and Southern Georgia

Respondents who saw the ad were asked to rate how much they liked it on a 10-point scale.

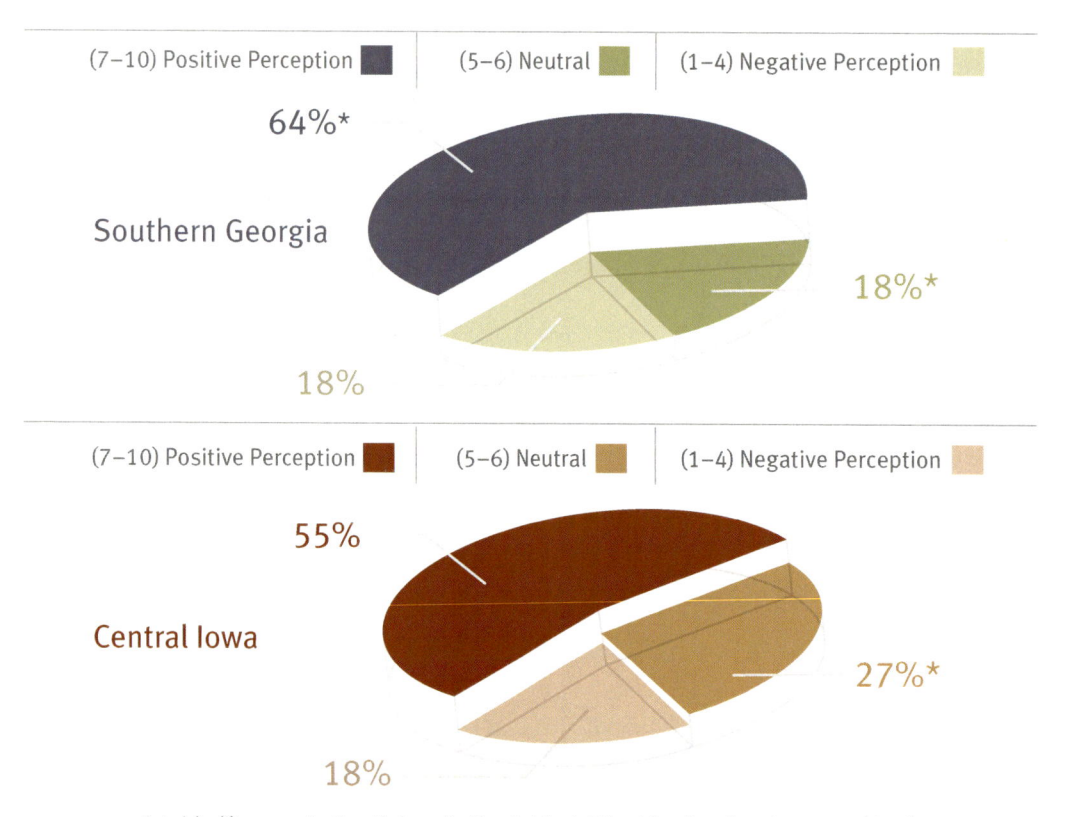

Southern Georgia
- (7–10) Positive Perception: 64%*
- (5–6) Neutral: 18%
- (1–4) Negative Perception: 18%*

Central Iowa
- (7–10) Positive Perception: 55%
- (5–6) Neutral: 27%*
- (1–4) Negative Perception: 18%

Asterisks (*) represent ratings that are significant at the 0.05 level (southern Georgia vs. central Iowa).
Source: *Geek the Library: A Community Awareness Campaign*, OCLC, 2011

Less than 20 percent of residents in each market rated the campaign negatively, and further investigation indicated that the negative associations fell into two main categories: those who did not like the word "geek" and/or did not like the use of the word as a verb, and those who did not understand the connection between the campaign and the library.

Although the details of the campaign message were not fully understood by all potential supporters in the pilot communities, the survey found that the campaign had begun to make an impact on some key perceptions and attitudes that indicated a stronger level of support for library funding, especially in southern Georgia.

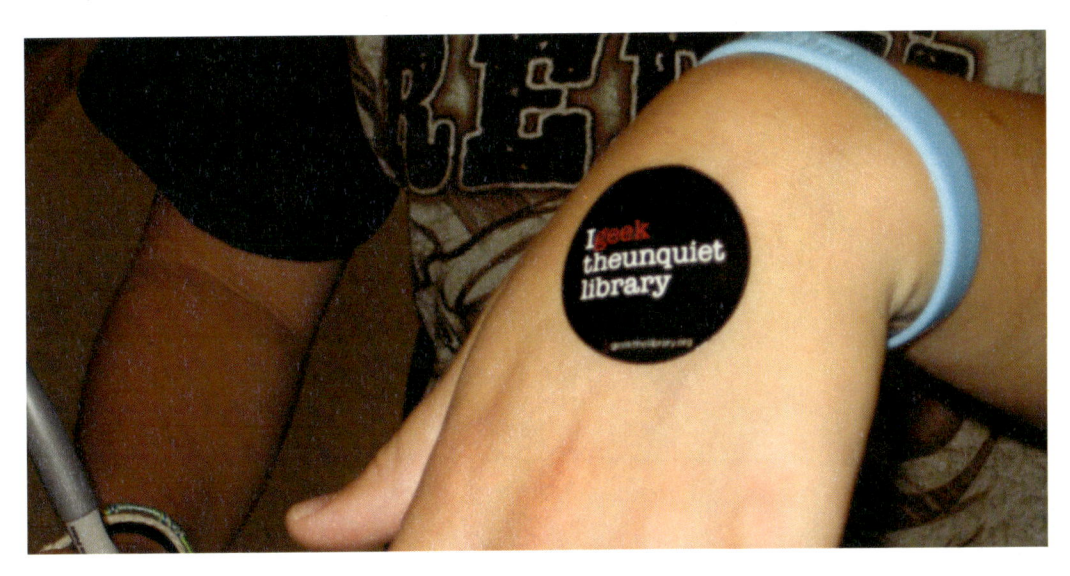

Additional observations from pilot libraries and from the field managers confirm that a large percentage of the public embraced the campaign and began to use "I geek" as part of their local vocabulary. For example, some local businesses and schools found ways to use the "geek" theme for their own programs and communications.

Raising awareness: Conclusion

The Geek the Library campaign gained impressive awareness for the short time in the market with 49 percent of residents in southern Georgia and 64 percent of residents in central Iowa recognizing it. The design had appeal, and advertising (e.g., newspaper ads and billboards) and public relations attracted attention: all helped build the foundation for the public to make the complete connection to the library and funding.

Step two: Changing perceptions

Based on the original research discussed in *From Awareness to Funding: A study of library support in America*, the Geek the Library awareness campaign had a goal to shift potential supporter perceptions along five key trajectories.

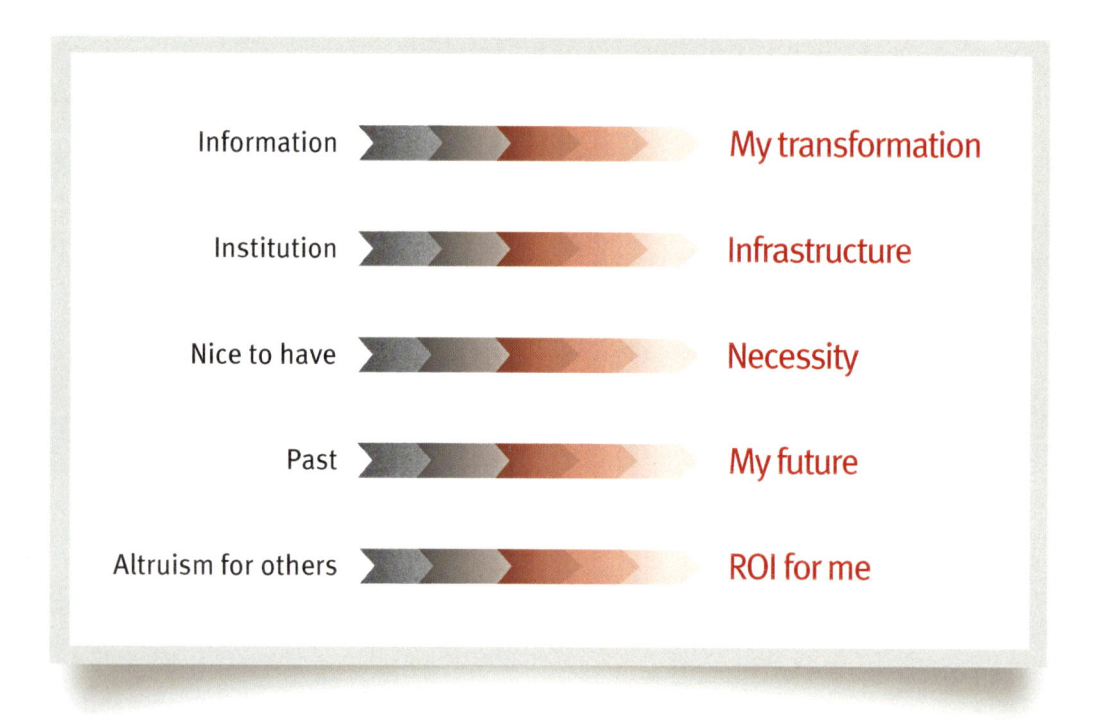

From	To
Information	My transformation
Institution	Infrastructure
Nice to have	Necessity
Past	My future
Altruism for others	ROI for me

In order to measure progress against those perceptual shifts, the pre- and post-campaign surveys asked residents if they agreed or disagreed (based on a 10-point scale) with roughly 40 different attitudes and perceptions related to the library, librarians and library funding. Examples include:

Information ▶ My transformation

The library empowers you.

The library enhances or rounds out your education.

The library inspires a love of learning.

The library is a place for anyone to explore their personal passion.

Institution ▶ ▶ **Infrastructure**

The library serves a serious purpose.

The library is an important cause that needs community support.

The library is still important and valuable in the Internet age.

Nice to have ▶ ▶ **Necessity**

The library is an indispensable part of the community.

The library is a valuable resource for everyone, no matter what their passion.

It's absolutely essential for every community to have access to a public library.

Past ▶ ▶ **My future**

The library allows everyone to pursue personal and professional passions and interests.

Having a top-notch public library is very important.

The librarians at the local public library are true advocates for lifelong learning.

Altruism ▶ ▶ **Return on investment**

The library is well worth the money that the community invests in it.

If the library in my community were to shut down, something essential and important would be lost, affecting the entire community.

In tough economic times, the public library is even more valuable to the community.

Changing perceptions: Southern Georgia

The results of the post-campaign tracking survey indicated that the campaign had a positive impact on several key perceptions and attitudes in southern Georgia. Not only did potential supporters show high levels of campaign awareness (49 percent of residents were familiar with the campaign), but there was evidence of statistically significant shifts in some of the key perceptions and attitudes relating to libraries, librarians and library funding.

Respondents in southern Georgia were asked about 40 library perceptions and attitudes. The results indicated positive movement in several attitudes and perceptions likely to impact long-term support for libraries.

Perceptions and attitudes around the library's importance and value improved

Southern Georgia

	Pre-wave	Post-wave
The public library serves a serious purpose.	69%	75%*
The public library enhances or rounds out your education.	57%	65%*
The librarians at the local public library are true advocates for lifelong learning.	55%	63%*
It is important to support the public library.	65%	72%*
The public library is well worth the money that the community invests in it.	63%	72%*
I would definitely vote for a referendum that would raise taxes in order to better fund the public library.	33%	40%*

Percentage of respondents who agree. Asterisks (*) represent ratings significant at the 0.05 level (pre- vs. post-wave).
Source: *Geek the Library: A Community Awareness Campaign*, OCLC, 2011

Each of these perceptions and attitudes is related strongly to the repositioning of the library from information to transformation, from institution to community infrastructure, from a 'nice-to-have' to a necessity.

The belief that the librarians at the local library are true advocates for lifelong learning is also one of the key attributes making up the 'Passionate Librarian' as discussed in the report *From Awareness to Funding: A study of library support in America*. (Chapter One of this report includes a set of perceptions that are highly correlated to library support.)

The changes in the perceived value of the library and the librarian are accompanied by a greater number of potential supporters who would definitely vote for an increase in taxes to fund the public library (33 percent vs. 40 percent).

While willingness to fund the libraries increased in southern Georgia, the same isn't true for all government services. Respondents were asked about their willingness to increase taxes to fund a variety of public services, including police, fire department and schools in addition to the public library. The public library was the only public service that experienced a statistically significant increase in the number of residents willing to increase their support.

The percentage of residents who definitely agree with increasing taxes to support library funding increased significantly when compared with other services

Southern Georgia

Respondents who agree they would support an increase in taxes in order to better fund…

	Pre-wave	Post-wave
…the public library	33%	40%*
…the school system	49%	48%
…the fire department	44%	46%
…the police department	39%	46%

Percentage of respondents who agree. (Respondents were prompted with various options.)
Asterisks (*) represent ratings significant at the 0.05 level (pre- vs. post-wave).
Source: *Geek the Library: A Community Awareness Campaign*, OCLC, 2011

Libraries across the country will likely continue to face difficult decisions due to continued budget cuts and funding challenges, at least in the near term. Meanwhile, the value that public libraries provide to the community is increasingly clear during the current economic downturn. The results of the pilot in southern Georgia indicate that the campaign has the potential to make a difference to improve people's attitudes toward libraries and library support in a relatively short time period.

Stories from pilot libraries reinforced the potential for the campaign to have immediate impact. Pilot library staff reported meeting community members who simply didn't know that the library was in need and didn't have a clear understanding of what they could do. The campaign helped educate residents about how funding works and provide constructive advice about how every individual can make a positive impact.

Changing perceptions: Central Iowa

In central Iowa, the impact of the campaign in potential supporters' perceptions and attitudes was different to that in southern Georgia. Although the level of campaign awareness in central Iowa surpassed those in southern Georgia (64 percent compared to 49 percent of residents were aware of the Geek the Library campaign), changes in perceptions and attitudes measured were minimal. The one attitude that changed significantly indicated simply that people were paying more attention to the library.

It is not unusual for different markets to have unique results during the testing of a pilot campaign as there are always a number of distinct factors at play. This can be due to specific environmental factors (economics, politics, competing campaigns), and/or can indicate that a greater level of investment and time is required to impact perceptions and behavior.

In order to explore potential influencing factors, a second phase of messaging was implemented in both southern Georgia and central Iowa in the spring of 2010. This additional messaging reinforced the connection between the campaign, the critical and transformational services libraries provide, and the need for funding those efforts.

Following the second phase of the campaign, an additional post-tracking study was conducted in central Iowa only. Telephone interviews with 396 residents were conducted April 23–29, 2010.

Additional post-tracking study: Central Iowa

The results of this second post-tracking study indicated that awareness of the campaign remained high (although the level of investment in the additional messaging was significantly less than the first round). In addition, two key perceptions had changed, both of which have the potential over time to positively impact support for public library funding.

The results of the second post-tracking study indicated that the core message and the associated perception that libraries "help you pursue your passions and interests" had increased significantly. Results of the first tracking study in both central Iowa and southern Georgia indicated that a small number of residents had not clearly understood the message of the campaign. The second survey in Iowa, however, indicated that this was more clearly understood after introduction of the additional messaging.

After the second phase of messaging, more residents in central Iowa had the perception that the library allows you to pursue your passions and interests

Central Iowa

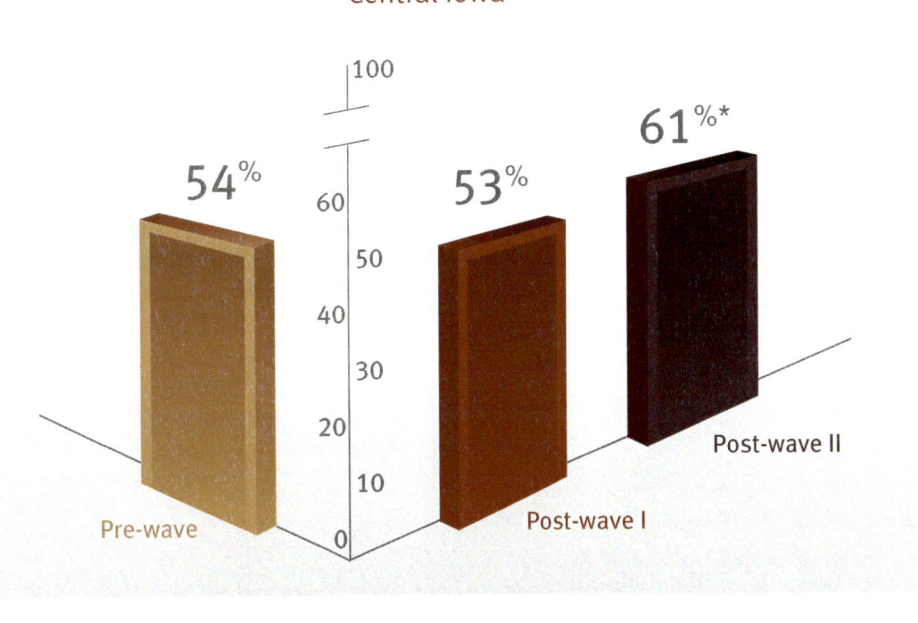

- Pre-wave: 54%
- Post-wave I: 53%
- Post-wave II: 61%*

Percentage of respondents who agree that the library allows them to pursue their passions and interests.
Asterisks (*) represent ratings significant at the 0.05 level (pre-wave vs. post-wave II).
Source: *Geek the Library: A Community Awareness Campaign*, OCLC, 2011

During the second post-tracking survey, central Iowa residents were asked a number of questions exploring any local factors that might either positively or negatively impact library perceptions and support for library funding, influencing the results of the campaign pilot. Respondents heard six statements and answered if they agreed or disagreed that each was true.

- All publicly funded organizations seem to need more money lately and it's difficult to choose which ones should get more.

- There's been a lot of political debate between publicly funded organizations within the last six months.

- My community supports its libraries and schools more than the typical community.

- Within the last six months, there have been tax referendums or other specific measures for police, etc., that have drawn local attention and debate.

- Within the last six months, I've seen articles about library-related issues.

- The libraries in my area have enough funding and should be able to make do.

Respondents were also asked how believing each statement would affect the likelihood of voting for a referendum that would raise taxes to better fund the library. The results indicated that residents overall had strong levels of agreement with these statements ranging from 85 percent down to 48 percent, but in most cases their belief would make them more likely to vote for library funding or make no change. The only belief that was likely to decrease library funding support was the belief that libraries already have enough funding, held by 48 percent of respondents.

Respondents were asked if there were any other factors likely to decrease library funding support and over 75 percent said no. The remaining factors mentioned were diverse and no single item stood out as an additional influencing factor.

Nearly half of surveyed residents believe their local libraries have enough funding

Central Iowa

Respondents were asked how each statement would affect the likelihood of voting for a referendum that would raise taxes to better fund the library.

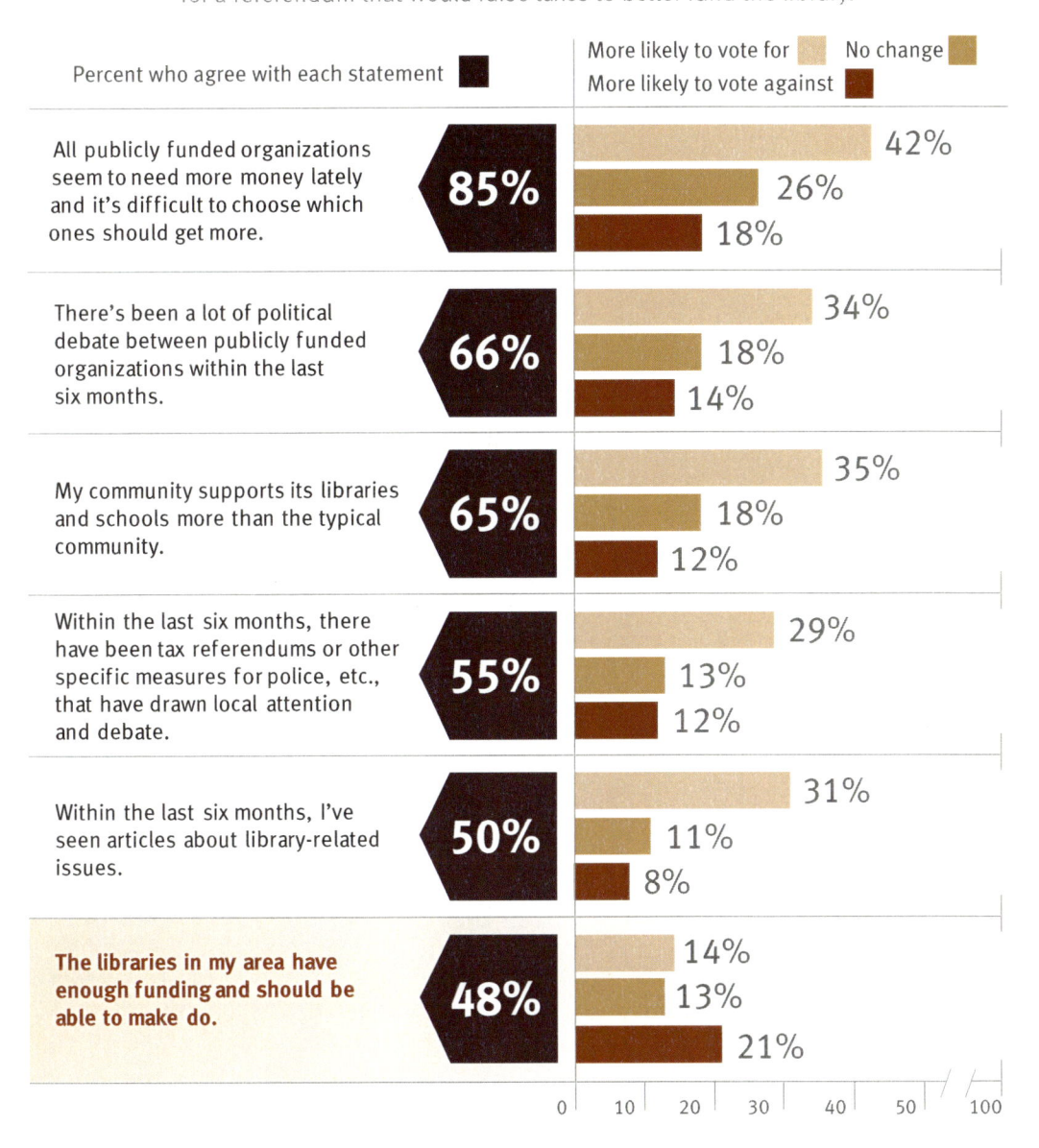

Percent who agree with each statement ■
More likely to vote for ▨ No change ▨
More likely to vote against ▨

Statement	Percent agree	More likely to vote for	No change	More likely to vote against
All publicly funded organizations seem to need more money lately and it's difficult to choose which ones should get more.	85%	42%	26%	18%
There's been a lot of political debate between publicly funded organizations within the last six months.	66%	34%	18%	14%
My community supports its libraries and schools more than the typical community.	65%	35%	18%	12%
Within the last six months, there have been tax referendums or other specific measures for police, etc., that have drawn local attention and debate.	55%	29%	13%	12%
Within the last six months, I've seen articles about library-related issues.	50%	31%	11%	8%
The libraries in my area have enough funding and should be able to make do.	48%	14%	13%	21%

Percentage of respondents who agree with each statement and say it makes them more likely to vote for or against a library referendum.
Source: *Geek the Library: A Community Awareness Campaign*, OCLC, 2011

The second important perception that changed in central Iowa in the second post-tracking survey was the perception that the local public library does not have sufficient money for day-to-day operations.

More residents believed that their local library had insufficient funding for day-to-day operations

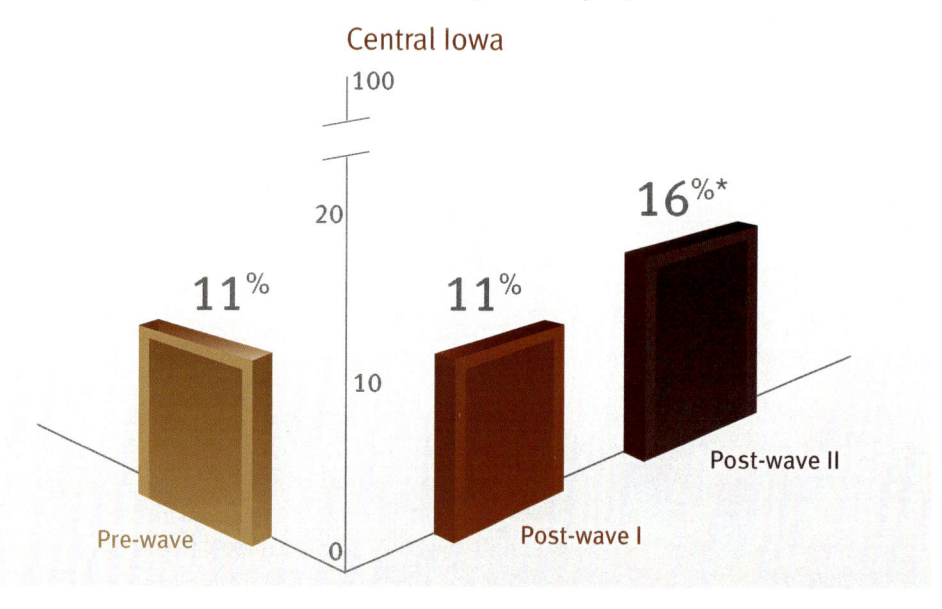

Central Iowa

- Pre-wave: 11%
- Post-wave I: 11%
- Post-wave II: 16%*

Percentage of respondents who agree that their local library had insufficient funding for day-to-day operations. Asterisk (*) represents ratings significant at the 0.05 level (pre-wave vs. post-wave II).
Source: *Geek the Library: A Community Awareness Campaign*, OCLC, 2011

This change is noteworthy since residents' perceptions about sufficient library funding is related to how they may vote in a referendum. However, it is important to recognize that despite the statistically significant increase in the number of residents concerned about funding for library operations, this still represents only 16 percent of the population.

The combination of results from the post-tracking studies in central Iowa indicate that in order for the campaign to have stronger impact on perceptions and attitudes relating to libraries and library support, more must be done to educate the public about the funding reality in the local community. This should occur alongside a continued emphasis on the important ways that the public library is helping support transformation of local residents and communities.

It is also important to note that central Iowa started with a significantly lower baseline for library funding support than southern Georgia. In southern Georgia, 38 percent of people said they would definitely support a referendum for the public library compared to 28 percent in central Iowa. This reinforces the reality that the implementation of the Geek the Library campaign in central Iowa, and other similar markets, will require a long-term commitment, with consistent engagement and communication with the community as a whole.

Changing perceptions: Conclusion

In southern Georgia, Geek the Library was successful at significantly changing a number of key attitudes and perceptions relating to the value of the public library, the role of the local librarian, and the value of the investment made by the community in the public library. There was a clear increase in willingness to support the library, including an increase in the number of residents who would definitely be willing to have their taxes raised. The changes in perceptions and attitudes in central Iowa were fewer, and indicated that more time, and a clearer understanding of the library funding need, would be required for long-term impact of the campaign in that market.

Step three: Driving behavior

The pilot campaign successfully achieved a very high level of awareness in a short period of time in both markets. More than half of all surveyed residents noticed the ads—they found them unique, interesting and likable. It also had a positive impact on many key perceptions about the library, especially in southern Georgia.

The ultimate measure of the campaign's success was whether it had the ability to impact behavior—specifically the types of behavior that would lead to an improvement in the library funding situation. Given the short timeframe, the Geek the Library team did not expect to see direct impact on funding-related behavior. Instead, the research looked at the following indicators to gauge the likelihood that the campaign would ultimately drive action:

- Short-term actions in direct response to the campaign, including direct engagement with the local library, increased conversations with friends and family and signing up to find out more

- Hypothetical response to the scenario where the local public library was facing significant cuts in funding

- Overall intent to vote in favor of increased library funding in the event of a referendum or ballot measure.

Residents in both markets showed levels of immediate action in response to the campaign that were significantly beyond expectations. The post-campaign survey asked respondents whether they had taken action or intended to take action in a wide variety of ways. Over two-thirds of residents in both southern Georgia and central Iowa had responded or intended to respond in one or more ways to the campaign.

The goal of the library pilot campaign was not to drive library usage, but it was not surprising that roughly a third of residents visited their local library in response to the campaign. The campaign put the spotlight on the library and, as an added benefit, served as a reminder about the library's mission to support every community member, no matter what their passion. The campaign inspired many residents to come in or visit the library's Web site. (Roughly 30 percent in each market visited their local library and roughly 15 percent in each market visited the library Web site in response to the campaign.)

Over two-thirds of people took action or intend to take action in response to the campaign

Southern Georgia and central Iowa

Southern Georgia	Central Iowa	Action
27%	32%	1. Visited my local library
24%*	14%	2. Have been talking to my friends/family more about the library
16%	15%	3. Visited Web site for local library
8%	16%*	4. Have been talking about Geek the Library ads
7%	7%	5. Visited geekthelibrary.org
7%	7%	6. Donated time or money to the local library
6%	10%	7. Attended an event at the local library
3%	3%	8. Took the survey on geekthelibrary.org
3%	2%	9. Contacted an elected official to express support for library
1%	1%	10. Signed up for the Geek the Library newsletter or e-mail
1%	2%	11. Bought a t-shirt or other item branded Geek the Library
11%	6%	Haven't done anything yet, but plan to

71% Southern Georgia
69% Central Iowa

Did at least one of the 11 actions or intends to

Percentage of respondents who have taken or intend to take each action.
Asterisks (*) represent ratings significant at the 0.05 level (southern Georgia vs. central Iowa).
Source: *Geek the Library: A Community Awareness Campaign*, OCLC, 2011

Geek the Library, and the hard work of pilot participants, were responsible for starting conversations about the library in both pilot markets. In southern Georgia, a quarter of respondents were talking more about the library to their friends and family. In central Iowa, residents were talking about the library (14 percent) and also about the campaign itself (16 percent). A number of people visited geekthelibrary.org (7 percent), signed up for e-mails (4 percent) or purchased campaign gear (1–2 percent), and 7 percent responded by contributing either time and/or money to their local library. The results found a small, but important, percentage of people (2–3 percent) who took the initiative to contact local elected officials to discuss the importance of the library to their communities.

Driving behavior: Southern Georgia

More than two-thirds of residents in southern Georgia reported taking some action in response to the Geek the Library campaign, including a quarter of respondents who indicated that they were talking more to their friends and family about the library.

During the post-campaign survey, respondents were also asked about their likely behavior in the case of two scenarios:

- First, how would they react if their local library faced significant funding cuts.

- Second, would they vote to increase taxes in support of public libraries.

The response to both of these scenarios in southern Georgia showed positive movement as a result of the Geek the Library campaign.

Respondents were asked how they would respond if their library budget was going to be cut significantly, and they were given a number of different alternative responses. From a comparison of the response during the post-campaign survey to that during the pre-campaign survey, there was an overall directional increase in the percentage of people who would respond in one or more ways, including contacting their local government. The percentage of residents whose response would include volunteering their time increased from 55 percent to 64 percent, a statistically significant change.

Response to library funding cuts showed improvement
Southern Georgia

Respondents were asked: How would you respond if your public library budget were going to be cut significantly?

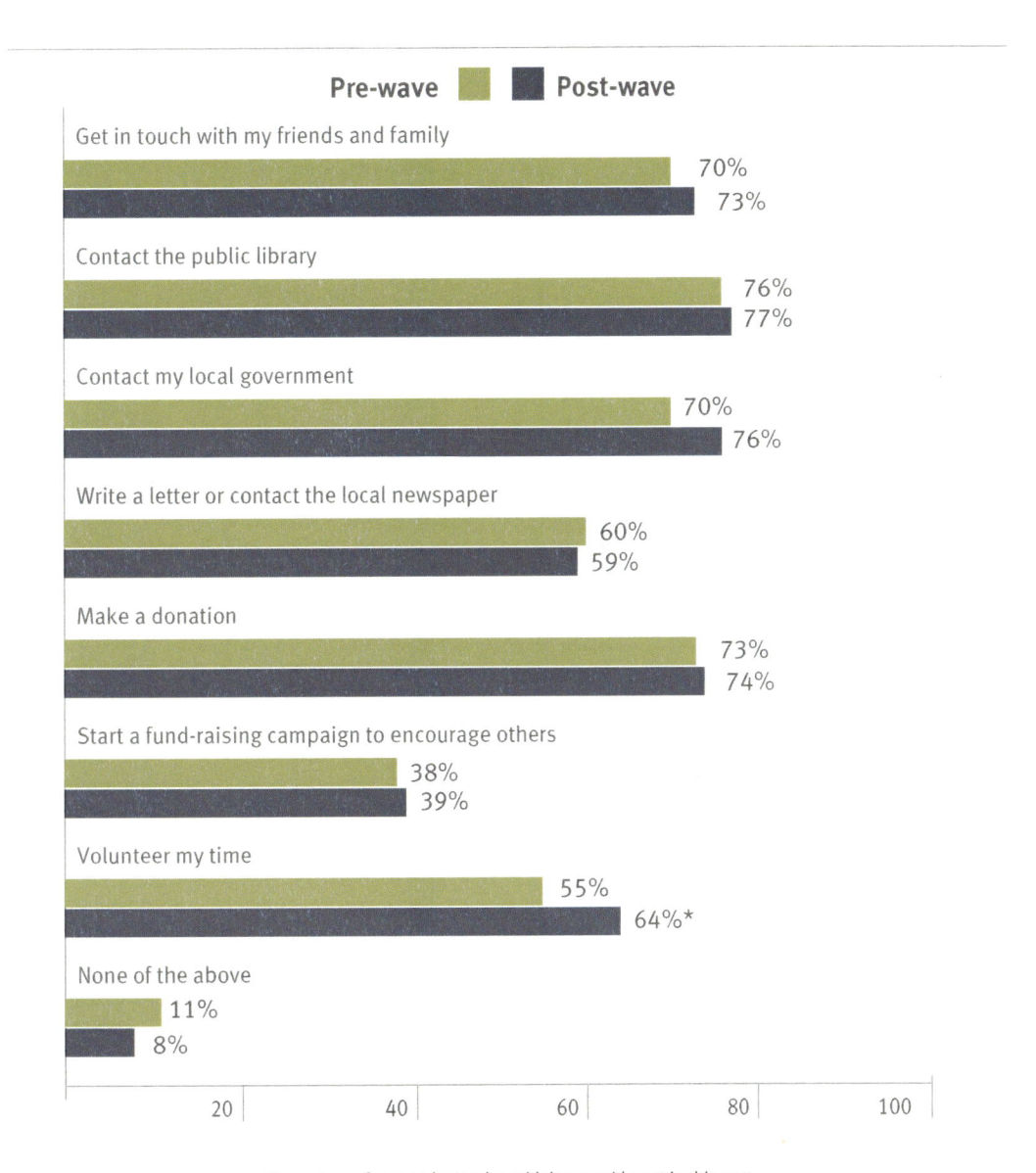

Pre-wave | **Post-wave**

Get in touch with my friends and family
- Pre-wave: 70%
- Post-wave: 73%

Contact the public library
- Pre-wave: 76%
- Post-wave: 77%

Contact my local government
- Pre-wave: 70%
- Post-wave: 76%

Write a letter or contact the local newspaper
- Pre-wave: 60%
- Post-wave: 59%

Make a donation
- Pre-wave: 73%
- Post-wave: 74%

Start a fund-raising campaign to encourage others
- Pre-wave: 38%
- Post-wave: 39%

Volunteer my time
- Pre-wave: 55%
- Post-wave: 64%*

None of the above
- Pre-wave: 11%
- Post-wave: 8%

Percentage of respondents who said they would react in this way.
Asterisks (*) represent ratings significant at the 0.05 level (pre- vs. post-wave).
Source: *Geek the Library: A Community Awareness Campaign*, OCLC, 2011

Geek the Library was successful in positively increasing the community's willingness to vote in favor of library funding. The public's intent to vote was measured in a number of ways during the survey. We have already reported that residents' overall willingness to raise taxes for the library had increased from 33 percent to 40 percent when asked in comparison with their attitudes toward funding a variety of public services.

The percentage of residents who definitely agreed with increasing taxes to support library funding increased significantly when compared with other services

Southern Georgia

Respondents who agree they would support an increase in taxes in order to better fund…

	Pre-wave	Post-wave
…the public library	33%	40%*
…the school system	49%	48%
…the fire department	44%	46%
…the police department	39%	46%

Percentage of respondents who agree. (Respondents were prompted with various options.)
Asterisks (*) represent ratings significant at the 0.05 level (pre- vs. post-wave).
Source: *Geek the Library: A Community Awareness Campaign*, OCLC, 2011

The survey also compared the degree of commitment to voting in favor of a library referendum before and after the campaign. In both surveys, respondents were asked about their likelihood to vote in favor of a public library funding measure—in response to this question, there was not a statistically significant change in the number of respondents saying they would definitely vote yes, but there was a significant shift from residents saying they may vote either way (27 percent to 21 percent) toward probably voting yes (29 percent to 36 percent).

Library support improved with voters moving from being on the fence to supporting a library ballot measure

Southern Georgia

Respondents were asked: Think ahead to the next election and assume that you are at the ballot box and ready to cast your vote. If there were a referendum, ballot initiative or bond measure for your local public library on the ballot, how do you think you would vote?

	Pre-wave	Post-wave
Definitely vote in favor of it.	38%	36%
Probably vote in favor of it.	29%	36% *
May vote either way.	27%	21% *
Probably vote against it.	3%	3%
Definitely vote against it.	2%	3%

Asterisks (*) represent ratings significant at the 0.05 level (pre- vs. post-wave).
Source: *Geek the Library: A Community Awareness Campaign*, OCLC, 2011

To complement these findings, the survey also evaluated the overall percentage of each community that would fall into the tiers of the library supporter segmentation from the original study (*From Awareness to Funding: A study of library support in America*). Although the results are directional only, they showed that there was a slight increase in the percentage of residents who would be classified as Super Supporters, indicating that the campaign may have moved some people from the Probable Supporter segment to be more committed library supporters.

Segments show some movement from Probable to Super Supporter

Southern Georgia

	Pre-wave	Post-wave
Super Supporters	12.7%	16.5%
Probable Supporters	43%	40.1%
Barriers to Support	26.7%	27%
Chronic Non Voters	17.6%	16.3%

Percentage of respondents in each segment.
Source: *Geek the Library: A Community Awareness Campaign*, OCLC, 2011

For reference:

- **Super Supporters:** Committed library supporters at the top tier of the segmentation pyramid.

- **Probable Supporters:** Voters who are likely to support library funding initiatives, but are not fully committed.

- **Barriers to Support:** Voters who, for a variety of factors, have significant barriers to voting in favor of increased library funding.

- **Chronic Non Voters:** People who are not registered to vote or have a history of choosing not to vote in presidential and local elections; they also indicate they are not likely to vote in the future, and are therefore unlikely to provide support for library funding initiatives.

Driving behavior: Central Iowa

Central Iowa experienced greater levels of campaign awareness than southern Georgia, but did not see the equivalent levels of change in perceptions and attitudes relating to libraries, librarians and library funding. It is not surprising, then, that the measures relating to willingness to support increased library funding remained static over the course of the pilot.

After a second round of messaging and a second post-campaign survey, results indicate that central Iowa residents were beginning to better understand the core transformational message of the campaign, and that there was more understanding that libraries do not have sufficient day-to-day funding, a perception that appeared to be a barrier to central Iowans' willingness to support increased library funding.

Level of voting intent remained virtually the same

Central Iowa

Respondents were asked: Think ahead to the next election and assume that you are at the ballot box and ready to cast your vote. If there was a referendum, ballot initiative or bond measure for your local public library on the ballot, how do you think you would vote?

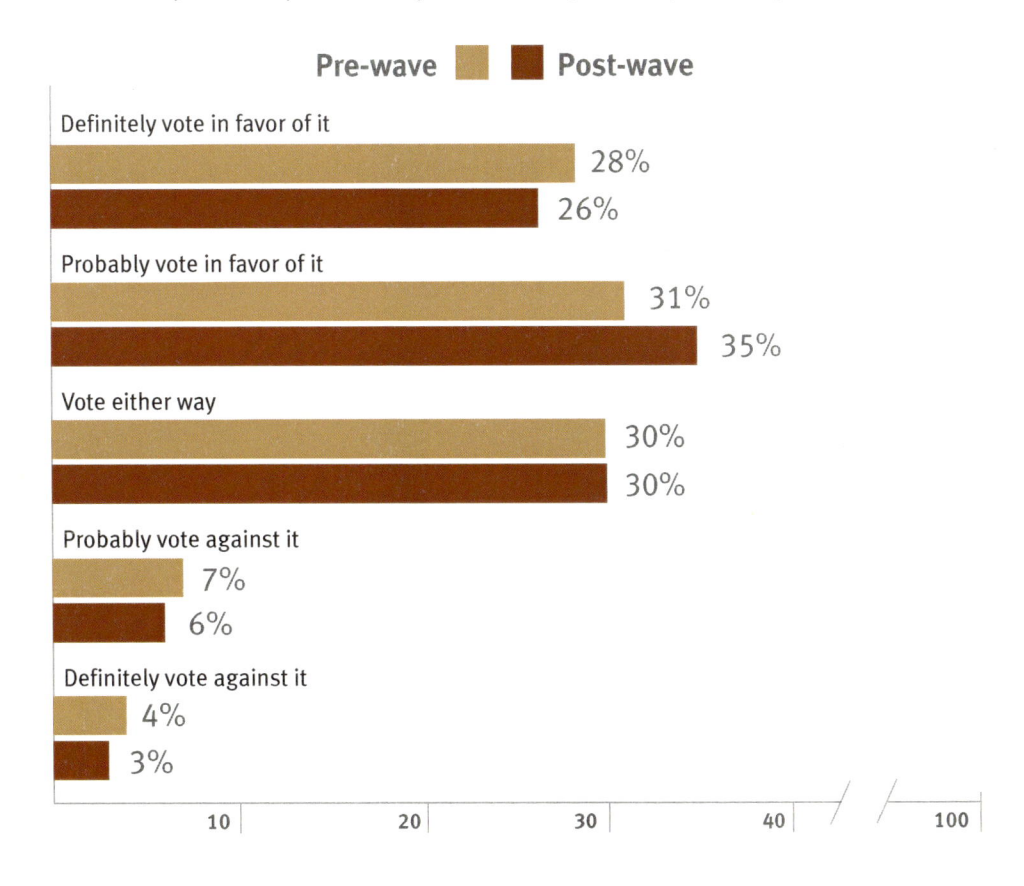

	Pre-wave	Post-wave
Definitely vote in favor of it	28%	26%
Probably vote in favor of it	31%	35%
Vote either way	30%	30%
Probably vote against it	7%	6%
Definitely vote against it	4%	3%

Source: *Geek the Library: A Community Awareness Campaign*, OCLC, 2011

Driving behavior: Conclusion

Geek the Library proved effective at driving positive library support behavior with over two-thirds of residents in both southern Georgia and central Iowa taking some action in response to seeing the campaign. Behavior changes directly relating to library funding—especially voting intent—improved in southern Georgia. For example, the percentage of residents who said they would be more likely to increase taxes to support the library and the percentage of residents who would probably vote in favor of a library referendum increased in southern Georgia. Again, these results indicate that the implementation of Geek the Library in Iowa (which started with a significantly lower baseline for library funding support than southern Georgia) and similar markets requires a long-term commitment to see significant results.

Summary

Overall, both markets showed notable changes in key elements of public awareness, attitudes and behavior relating to the public library and public library funding, much of which was more than expected in such a short time period. The campaign, and the incredible efforts of pilot library leaders and staff, helped educate, inform and motivate the public. The important conversations and active behavioral shifts resulting from enthusiastically engaging residents, and the important advocacy lessons learned by the pilot libraries during the campaign, made an impact in the short term and will hopefully continue to positively influence library funding through proactive public engagement and education in the pilot markets. Many pilot participants also reported local success stories, such as increased local support from key decision makers, all of which may have been influenced by campaign efforts.

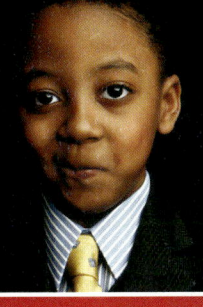

Geek the Library in Action

Chapter 4

Wegeekideas

The Geek the Library pilot campaign learnings were not limited to the results of the quantitative tracking study. Enthusiastic pilot library leaders and staff provided rich insights and helpful examples about the experience of implementing the campaign in their local communities.

It was the steadfast commitment of these passionate participants that drove overall campaign impact. We are extremely proud and appreciative of their efforts and the local results. This chapter showcases many of the strategies and tactics used by pilot libraries—including public relations and media outreach, advertising, community events and social media.

Passionate librarians make the difference

Geek the Library made an impact in pilot communities, but the pre- and post-campaign surveys tell only part of the story. The dedication and persistent efforts of library participants heavily influenced the positive changes in key public perceptions and behaviors relating to the library, librarians and public library support.

Pilot library activities were measured and evaluated in a number of ways, including tracking of Web site hits and other online activities, local community event attendance, article placements in newspapers and other media, and direct information from participating libraries. These ongoing measures provided additional insights about the effectiveness of specific campaign activities, and the importance of the local library's role in making the Geek the Library campaign a success.

Dedicated staff and supportive library leaders were the driving force for the overall effectiveness of each local campaign. The pilot experience confirmed that success with Geek the Library depends on not one or two specific promotional elements, but the effective implementation of all facets of the campaign: advertising and public relations, community events and grassroots programs, Web sites and social networking.

It's important to note that the second group of pilot libraries, added after the initial launch in June 2009, did not have the same robust advertising strategy or financial support as the initial libraries in central Iowa and southern Georgia. As a result, these libraries spent significant time planning their launch approaches and overall strategies, and relied heavily on community events, grassroots efforts and public relations initiatives. Less advertising dollars inspired creativity and resourcefulness. We also found that having direct control of the amount and placement of advertising helped these libraries successfully tailor the campaign to each unique community.

Advertising

Geek the Library advertising initiates interest, and presents the library as relevant and vital.

Advertising efforts in the pilot communities were an important success factor for educating community members and thereby raising awareness. (The initial group of pilot libraries in southern Georgia and central Iowa received full support from OCLC with advertising strategy and implementation.)

The results of the pre- and post-campaign surveys measured awareness at the beginning and end of the pilot, but the pilot libraries knew that advertising efforts were having an impact early on, as members of the public came into the library to ask about the campaign. Billboards and other signage acted as a catalyst for these conversations. Billboards were placed in high-traffic areas and the visual impact drew attention. The results of the campaign tracking study indicated that the billboards were the most visible aspect of the advertising program (nearly 70 percent of people who saw the campaign in each market reported seeing the billboards) and they acted as a teaser for the public, who needed to see other aspects of the campaign to find out more.

The advertising programs in southern Georgia and central Iowa included newspaper, radio and online advertising, in addition to the billboards and other signage. Advertising effectiveness is measured by the number of impressions (number of times a person will see a campaign ad) and the reach of the advertising (the percentage of the community residents who will have seen at least one aspect of the campaign).

Based on advertising industry standards for measuring advertising impressions and reach, the Geek the Library campaign reached 97 percent of the population in southern Georgia and central Iowa, and generated an estimated 127,688,880 impressions:

- Advertising impressions for central Iowa: 67,238,650 (goal = 50,057,622)
- Advertising impressions for southern Georgia: 60,450,230 (goal = 46,765,820)

Pilot library participants, especially those who were responsible for planning their own advertising strategies, contributed to overall advertising efforts in many creative ways by identifying effective promotional channels.

Bright ideas and best practices

Des Moines Public Library in Iowa partnered with Des Moines Water Works to include Geek the Library handouts in a monthly mailing. There was no cost to the library for the mailing. The library simply provided the printed handouts.

Milwaukee Public Library in Wisconsin created an original TV commercial using library staff and members of the community that was tied to the 2010 Winter Olympics. The ad was part of a sponsorship package for local coverage of the event. Milwaukee Public Library also advertised on bus stop shelters.

Piedmont Public Library and several other participating libraries in southern Georgia and central Iowa identified local access or cable TV stations that ran the campaign videos as commercials.

Public relations and media outreach

Geek the Library provides new opportunities to build or strengthen relationships with local media.

Existing relationships between pilot libraries and local media channels were key to making the pilot campaign launch a success. Many of the media outlets that ran Geek the Library advertising also offered value-add opportunities as part of the advertising buy, such as interviews and campaign coverage. Articles in the local newspapers and interviews with local television and radio were important complements to advertising in helping to reach a large percentage of the pilot communities at campaign launch and beyond.

Local libraries helped compile lists of important local media contacts and worked with the Geek the Library team to distribute campaign press materials. Local media were invited to attend launch events, and the team provided Geek the Library goody bags filled with giveaways and high-level information about the campaign and its educational purpose.

Following the initial launch, participating libraries and the Geek the Library team found several ways to keep the campaign and the story behind the campaign in the media. Successful strategies included letters to the editor from library supporters, including Friends of the Library and library board members, and introducing the media to local transformational library stories. The Geek the Library campaign pilot achieved nearly 300 placements in total across all markets, including major newspapers, major network TV affiliates, print, radio and online media (blogs).

Bright ideas and best practices

Des Moines Public Library and Ames Public Library in central Iowa were active in supporting the pilot launch, with a total of 14 interviews with local media during launch week alone. **Des Moines Public Library** coordinated an interview about the campaign with the mayor of Des Moines, Frank Cownie, for the Mayor's Spotlight on the city's local cable access channel, DMTV.

Hog Hammock Public Library, part of Three Rivers Library System in southern Georgia, consistently utilized local newspaper announcements to promote library events, and the branch manager wrote a letter to the editor sharing the key elements of the awareness campaign.

Live Oak Public Libraries launched the southern Georgia pilot in Savannah with an outdoor event in Johnson Square. The launch team, including the Live Oak marketing staff, promoted the event in local newspaper listings and through Live Oak's established communication channels. The location and timing of the event, in an area of Savannah that many residents walk through during the day, ensured that the campaign launch had impact. Over 700 people attended the event, which lasted from 10 a.m. to 1 p.m. The launch was covered by key television, radio and print outlets, with a total of 29 interviews and articles, in addition to blog and Twitter posts.

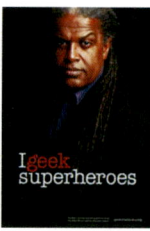

Richmond Hill Public Library in southern Georgia was a library that had not previously worked much with local media. Its staff supplied Geek the Library educational materials to *Richmond Hill Reflections* magazine. The resulting article educated readers about the significant role their library plays in their community and the funding challenges faced by the library.

As part of community-based educational efforts, **Story County, Iowa** library leaders presented a Geek the Library t-shirt to Iowa Governor Chet Culver, accompanied him on his Iowa Unlimited Whistle Stop Train Tour, and talked to him about the value of public libraries and library funding. The press took photos and covered the story.

Community events

Geek the Library is an effective vehicle for getting out into the community, and attending new and diverse local events.

Community events provided a fun and easy way for the pilot library staff to engage with members of their individual communities. There were many local opportunities and the Geek the Library theme was easily tailored to fit specific festivals and activities. The visual impact of campaign banners and table skirts helped draw attention, and the public lined up to pick up posters, stickers, bookmarks and bags.

The biggest attraction at many events was what became known as the geek wall—a large, free-standing wall that people could write on to share what they geek. At some events, local photographers took people's photos with the wall and photos were posted on the campaign Flickr group page. People signed a release to permit their photos to be posted.

At smaller events, libraries found an inexpensive and more mobile solution to the geek wall with black foam core panels, a 'What do you geek?' bumper sticker, portable easels and silver markers. Event attendees were just as eager to share what they geek and the panels were then placed on display at the library. Library staff and volunteers enjoyed the opportunity to engage with the public, and found that it was easy to talk about the campaign and its purpose—to educate and raise awareness of the valuable services provided by libraries and the need for library funding.

Several pilot libraries also held events at the library, and used the campaign materials and theme to promote attendance. In some cases, these were library events that were already on the library calendar, and in other cases they were created specifically as part of the library's Geek the Library marketing plan.

Bright ideas and best practices

Bertha Bartlett Public Library in central Iowa participated in the Story City storytelling festival, a three-day event that features stories told by a variety of people around the city of Story City. The Geek the Library kiosk was a stop on the tour, and the library printed custom t-shirts that said, "I geek storytelling."

Bondurant Public Library in central Iowa entered a float featuring a large campaign banner in the annual Prairie Meadows Racetrack and Casino Parade and won second prize. The title was "Fables and Stables" and featured classic literary characters.

Okefenokee Regional Library System in Georgia organized walk-arounds at community events and parades to distribute Geek the Library goody bags and discuss public library funding.

Piedmont Regional Library System in Georgia participated in the systemwide Geek the Library week with a variety of activities. Campaign materials were distributed throughout the community. All 11 branches took part. Other pilot libraries hosted their own Geek the Library week, some with mayoral proclamations.

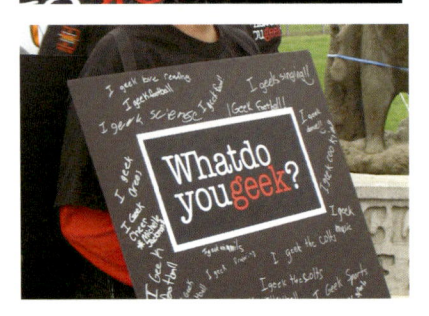

Shelbyville-Shelby County Public Library in Indiana launched its Geek the Library campaign at a local high school football game. Director Janet Wallace made sure she got the attention of the media and the public by wearing a mobile geek wall as a sandwich board.

Wayne County Library, part of Three Rivers Regional Library System in Georgia, took part in job fairs promoting Geek the Library. The library used these events to remind attendees of the resources available to help support online job searches, applications and resumé writing.

Zion-Benton Public Library in Illinois invited a variety of community leaders to the library and worked with a local photographer to create custom posters. The local 'movers and shakers' were invited to a follow-up breakfast where they learned about the campaign and received multiple copies of their posters to distribute in the community.

Web site, online tools and social media

Geek the Library encourages your community to engage online.

The campaign Web site, geekthelibrary.org, provides opportunities for visitors to find out more about the campaign, download educational materials, watch videos, and learn about local library funding and how they can lend support. The Web site also incorporates a simple poll and the ability to sign up for e-mail messages.

One of the most popular areas of the Web site is the 'Get Your Geek On' section (geekthelibrary.org/getyourgeekon), where library staff and supporters can share what they geek and how the library supports them. Over the course of the pilot, hundreds of people shared what they geek, with passions ranging from guitars to baking. All the geeks are combined to form a virtual geek wall.

caitlingeekshistory
I've always been in love with history. I'm good at it, I find it fun and it makes sense to me. I've always agreed with Winston Churchill that we need to study history or it'll repeat. And, I just found out I may be eligible for an out-of-state history scholarship, while still in the 9th grade. To a college I want to go to. Life is stellar. Totally stellar.

davegeeksmusic
Whether I'm looking for some obscure song done by a 'one-hit wonder' from my high school days, the greatest hits of a favorite band or just trying to find something new, the library is the place to explore for music of all genres! Oh, and I can find weird sound effects and the perfect music for a romantic Italian dinner with my wife. That's amore!

laurageekslibraries
Out of all the things I considered geeking (Harry Potter, knitting, The Beatles, etc.), I chose what may seem like an easy out ... libraries. However, libraries are my passion and will eventually be my career. I'm starting my journey towards my MLIS this week and could not be more proud to be a part of this amazing community. Who else fights for literacy, intellectual freedom and the accessibility for information more than a librarian? Therefore, I geek libraries.

lilogeekscomputerengineering
I dropped out of high school when I was 14 years old, and never learned math. While I always had an interest in computing and electronics, my lack of formal education kept me from seriously pursuing those studies. With help from my local library and the many resources available there, I began to read and learn about computer science and mathematics. Ten years later, I'm shopping for Ph.D. programs in computer engineering!

The Geek the Library social media sites provide additional opportunities for people to engage, learn and share. Facebook, in particular, took the campaign message far beyond the pilot communities, and continues to help carry and expand the conversation about the value of the library and the need for support.

Many participating libraries used their Web sites and other social media sites, such as Facebook and Twitter, to promote the campaign and link to geekthelibrary.org.

Bright ideas and best practices

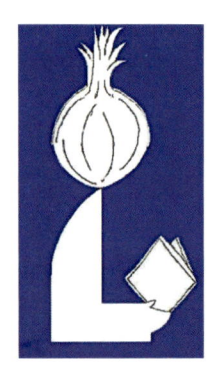

Many participants used Facebook, Twitter, Flickr and the help of local bloggers to update their communities about Geek the Library and to start a local public library funding conversation. **Ohoopee Regional Library System,** headquartered in Vidalia, Georgia, for example, recognized this vital communication avenue and posted regular Facebook status updates for the system's growing fan base—including many promoting Geek the Library during the pilot campaign. These activities helped spread the message beyond patrons.

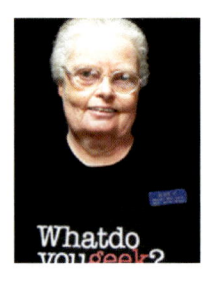

Shelbyville-Shelby County Public Library in Shelbyville, Indiana, took photos of staff—much like those from Geek the Library—and asked them what they geeked. The photos, along with their names, departments and number of years they've been with the library, were prominently featured on the library's homepage. The information was updated regularly, highlighting different staff members every week during the pilot campaign.

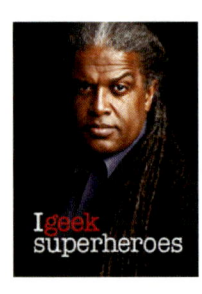

Participants utilized their library Web sites to promote Geek the Library in many different ways, but most often they used online banners featuring Geek the Library images and/or messages. Consistent use of these standard banners helped drive community traffic to geekthelibrary.org, and encouraged further interest in Geek the Library and public library funding. A banner added by **Live Oak Public Libraries** was a top referring Web site back to geekthelibrary.org during the pilot campaign.

Over 13,000 fans were added to the official Geek the Library Facebook page during the pilot campaign, putting it in the top four percent of similar Facebook pages. Activity and fan discussion on Facebook surpassed expectations (with an average of 20 to 40 responses per post) and provided valuable data about the direction of public funding conversation and the viral nature of the Geek the Library campaign.

The Geek the Library photo stream was used as an 'eye on the campaign' with regular updates. Likewise, the Geek the Library group page had over 80 members by the end of the pilot campaign, with nearly 1,000 total images.

Over 800 people were following the campaign on Twitter by the end of the campaign pilot. Retweeting of campaign tweets and Geek the Library mentions were consistent and passionate, and helped the message spread outside of the pilot markets.

Connecting with the community

Geek the Library allows libraries to connect with the community in new and effective ways. Grassroots programs and tools helped ensure that all residents understood the campaign. These efforts also encouraged residents to spread the campaign messages among friends and family, and the rest of the community. When residents embraced Geek the Library, as they did in some of the pilot communities, the campaign took on a life of its own, which improved the overall impact. Many pilot libraries saw greater awareness when messages were being reinforced organically within the community and the message wasn't coming only from the library.

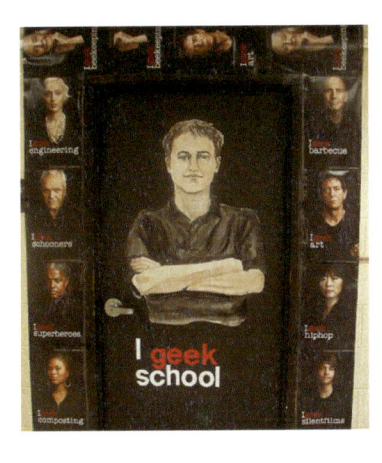

The primary purpose of the campaign posters was to take the message out to local businesses, restaurants and retailers, as well as to community organizations and schools, by asking them to display the posters in their windows or on their bulletin boards. This put the campaign in places that could reach potential supporters who may not be regular library users, while providing an opportunity for the library to build relationships with key community players. Posters were also a draw for local teachers, many of whom used them in their classrooms and built assignments around what the students geek. These efforts helped reinforce the community aspect of the campaign.

The pilot campaign included a number of tools for libraries to localize the messages. Poster templates, for example, were provided for pilot libraries to use with images of local people. Some libraries displayed the posters of local residents in the library, and found they would bring friends and relatives into the library to see them, providing an opportunity for dialogue.

Many participants used the Geek the Library postcards to help gain interest for the campaign. For example, to get the attention of influential members of the community, including elected officials, some libraries added preprinted educational messages and distributed them at events. Others used the postcards as invitations to events and as thank-you cards to top-tier supporters. The campaign also included several presentations and materials for libraries to use for sharing the campaign with local organizations, such as local chambers of commerce and Kiwanis chapters. Libraries found it effective to engage these groups as part of the launch and often combined the presentation with campaign giveaways.

Some of the most creative examples were libraries that integrated the campaign with existing community outreach programs.

Bright ideas and best practices

Appling County Public Library, part of Okefenokee Regional Library System in Georgia, worked with new mom programs at area hospitals. It provided Geek the Library goody bags and library materials, along with crocheted caps for the babies. Moms were reminded about the value of the library for the community and the great resources available.

Many pilot libraries partnered with local businesses, and asked them to distribute Geek the Library posters and other materials. But some businesses took the initiative on their own. A local retail establishment in Des Moines displayed a 'We Geek Warm Coats' sign. The staff from **Des Moines Public Library** followed up and asked them to give Geek the Library handouts to their customers.

Hog Hammock Public Library in southern Georgia is a small heritage library based on Sapelo Island off the Georgia coast and can be reached only by ferry. The manager featured posters around the community including on the Sapelo Island Ferry, multiple grocery stores and the Georgia State University branch located on the island.

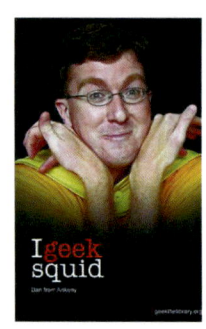

Kirkendall Public Library in Iowa was the first library to design and print custom Geek the Library posters featuring local people, including local celebrities. Nearly 30 posters were customized and printed for display, and then published online. The library also implemented a 'Geek of the Week' competition where the winning photo was displayed online every week.

Vidalia-Toombs County Library, part of Ohoopee Regional Library System in Georgia, leveraged its teen advisory board to implement and integrate the campaign. While teens were not a target audience, these young adults helped staff events and develop original campaign ideas—especially for the library Web site and social networking sites.

Connecting back to the library and to library funding

Geek the Library gets people talking and is a springboard for important local funding conversations.

The campaign design focuses heavily on community advocacy, and dissemination of educational material and marketing activities that reach potential supporters. But it is also important to make the connection from the campaign to the local library.

The pilot campaign included outdoor hanging banners that libraries could display on their buildings, depending on zoning laws, turning the library itself into a billboard for the campaign. Many libraries created displays that connected their materials and programs to the specific geeks featured in the campaign. Others found it easy to promote their programming by connecting the programs to the Geek the Library theme. Many pilot library leaders also leveraged the awareness developed by campaign activities by sharing the value of the library with local funding decision-making bodies.

Bright ideas and best practices

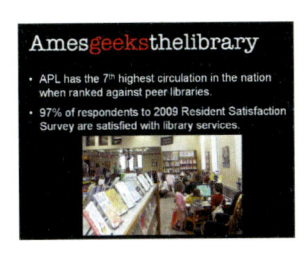

Ames Public Library in Iowa used the campaign as a launching pad to discuss the important need for continued funding with the Ames City Council. Director Art Weeks shared an educational PowerPoint presentation that explained the value the library provides to the community using the Geek the Library theme.

Richmond Hill Public Library in Georgia and many other pilot libraries created their own screensavers for library computers. Some used various static screensavers available on geekthelibrary.org, and others created unique and localized messages. Most reported increased interest in the campaign when using the screensavers.

Statesboro Regional Library System in Georgia captured a photo of its first newspaper ad insertion in the *Statesboro Herald* and embedded it in an e-mail directed to community leaders to announce the awareness campaign. Staff also developed local library funding charts to educate the public at events and in the library.

Waukee Public Library in Iowa found an effective way to create buzz about Geek the Library and encourage patrons to share what they geek. The library displayed a collection of employee photos featuring their own personal geeks.

Zion-Benton Public Library in Illinois went where the traffic was. Having already created a Ride & Read program at the train station that takes hundreds of people in and out of Chicago every day, staff decided to make this a Geek the Library opportunity with customized stickers.

Many pilot libraries created eye-catching displays within the library and at other locations around the community to get patrons asking questions and talking about the campaign. Some libraries were able to develop displays for local municipal buildings, civic centers and schools.

Summary

Participating library staff played a critical role in making the campaign meaningful and impactful in their communities. Getting out into the community consistently helped many library leaders and staff ensure that their communities learned about the value of libraries and the critical funding issues they face, and made the connection between the campaign and funding. Field observations and library feedback confirm that some participants considered this kind of community outreach—especially to influential members of the community, including public officials—unfamiliar territory, while others were comfortable in this role. The campaign gave them a vehicle to start community conversations.

It was clear that there were many distinct factors leading to individual library success. Factors included:

- Willingness to commit the resources necessary to execute a fully functioning local awareness campaign

- Creativity and engagement in funding ways to build on and localize the campaign

- Educating the community and connecting Geek the Library to the library's story
    - Explaining what 'geek' means and sharing the purpose of the campaign, and using the messages as launching pads for more detailed library funding discussions
    - Bridging the topics of usage and funding, and value and need

- Using the campaign to build or expand relationships between the library and the community, especially influential members of the community, including elected officials

- Encouraging spread of the campaign by taking advantage of the people and organizations closest to them, such as library support groups.

We thank the pilot library staff and leaders for their tremendous efforts and consistent feedback. Pilot participants said:

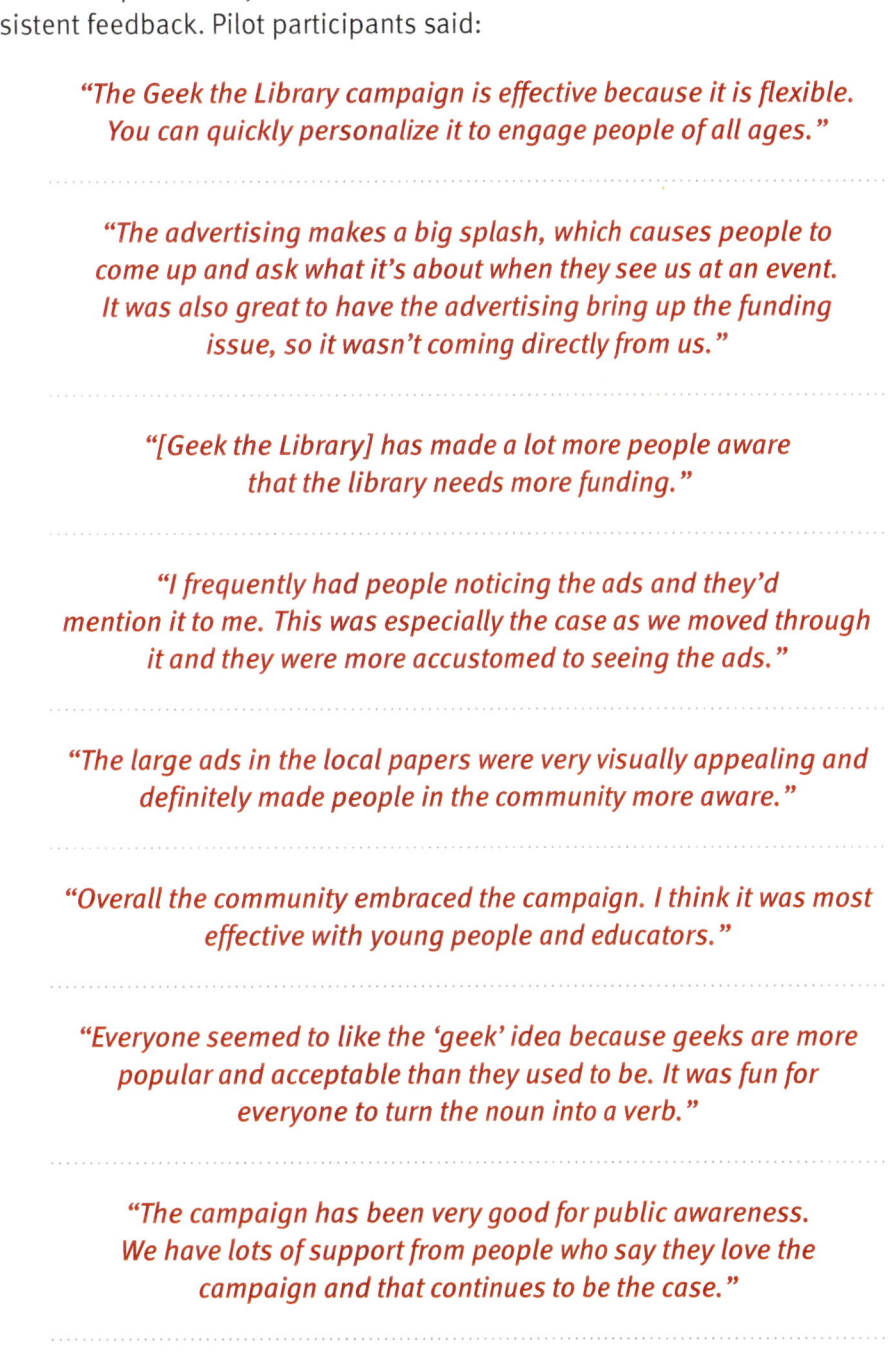

"The Geek the Library campaign is effective because it is flexible. You can quickly personalize it to engage people of all ages."

"The advertising makes a big splash, which causes people to come up and ask what it's about when they see us at an event. It was also great to have the advertising bring up the funding issue, so it wasn't coming directly from us."

"[Geek the Library] has made a lot more people aware that the library needs more funding."

"I frequently had people noticing the ads and they'd mention it to me. This was especially the case as we moved through it and they were more accustomed to seeing the ads."

"The large ads in the local papers were very visually appealing and definitely made people in the community more aware."

"Overall the community embraced the campaign. I think it was most effective with young people and educators."

"Everyone seemed to like the 'geek' idea because geeks are more popular and acceptable than they used to be. It was fun for everyone to turn the noun into a verb."

"The campaign has been very good for public awareness. We have lots of support from people who say they love the campaign and that continues to be the case."

> *"While I can't prove that Geek the Library helped generate additional funding for my library, I do know that my city council recently overwhelmingly moved to add additional funds to my library— funds that had been denied by the city administrator, but which the city council members restored. Perhaps Geek the Library was a motivating factor."*

> *"The Geek the Library campaign has given us invaluable knowledge about where advertisements are the most effective in our community. This has helped us when planning events and supplied data for grant applications."*

> *"[The community] thinks it was a very professional campaign and really eye-catching."*

The pilot participants' experiences paved the way for new libraries to successfully implement the campaign. Everything we learned during the pilot campaign informed development of materials and guides to help other libraries that adopt the campaign in the future. Geek the Library is currently open to all U.S. public libraries.

Get Geek the Library

Chapter 5

We geek libraries

We've tested the campaign, we've created the materials and now we've made Geek the Library available to all U.S. public libraries. Interested public libraries can go to get.geekthelibrary.org for detailed information about how the campaign works, staff and budget commitments, and the benefits for participating libraries and local communities. Libraries that decide to implement the campaign receive initial training and full access to all campaign material, including art templates and supplementary guides. This chapter provides insight about how to get involved and how the campaign can benefit your community.

Open to all U.S. public libraries

Libraries have the opportunity to localize this effective community awareness campaign to help their communities better understand the value of libraries and every individual's role in library funding. The campaign has the potential to affect positive consumer behavior relating to library support—including increasing the likelihood to vote for a library levy or referendum.

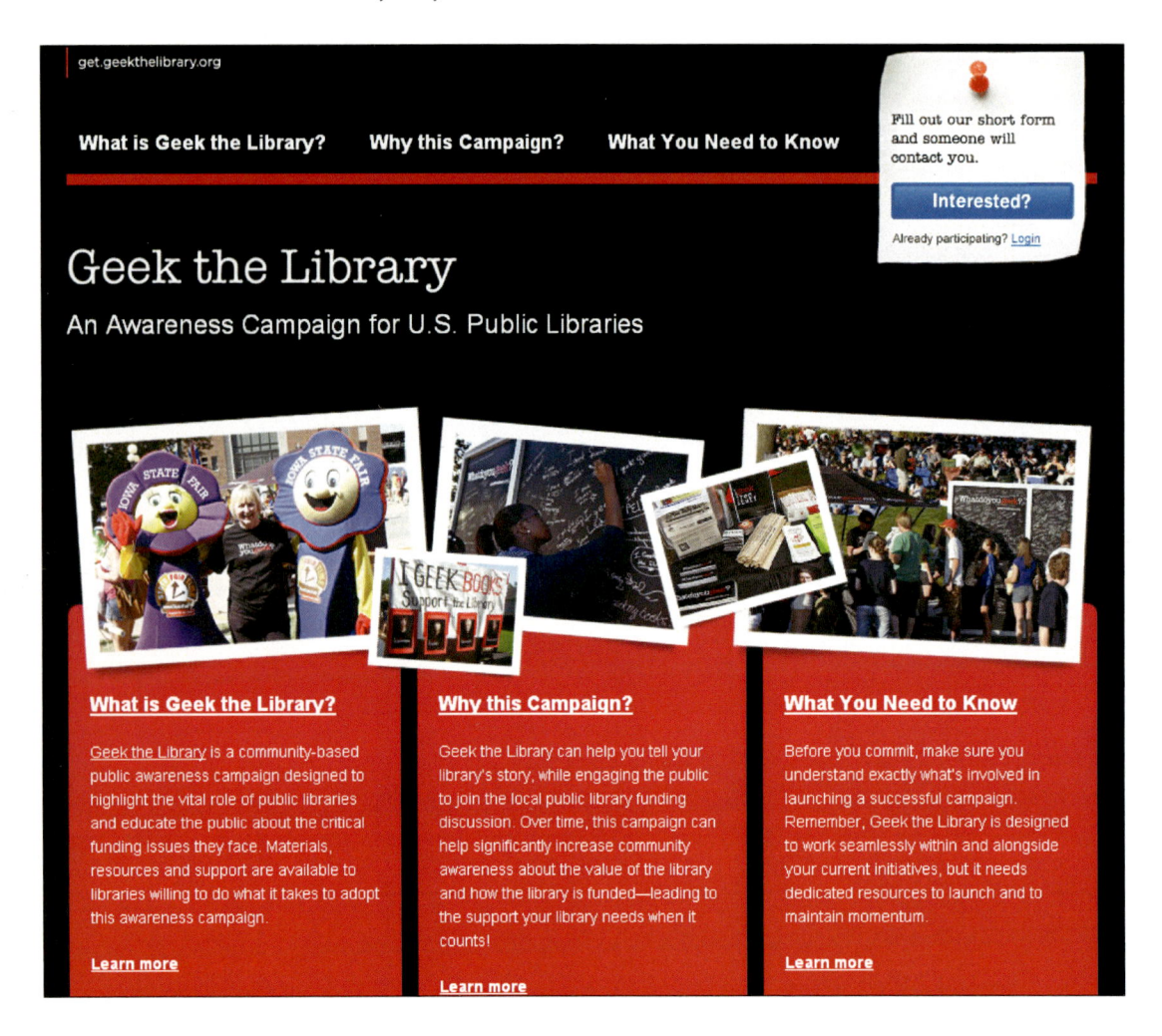

Detailed information about Geek the Library and how local implementation can provide many benefits is available on get.geekthelibrary.org. Libraries can submit a short online form, and a member of the Geek the Library team will personally call to answer any questions and discuss specific concerns. Libraries receive a kit with helpful materials, including a PowerPoint presentation to assist in introducing Geek the Library to key library stakeholders, such as library boards. A sample goody bag with various Geek the Library campaign materials, such as stickers and postcards, is also included.

A simple, online participation agreement must be 'agreed to' in order to launch the campaign.

Support and free materials

Each library and library system is unique. Geek the Library field managers provide important advice about how the campaign may unfold locally based on specific circumstances of each library and library system. Often, field managers can suggest collaborations between libraries within close proximity or provide marketing advice to help encourage key library stakeholder approval.

Libraries that decide to implement the campaign receive initial training and full access to all campaign material, including art templates and supplementary guides. A comprehensive online Campaign Management Center is a one-stop resource for implementing Geek the Library. This password-protected Web site includes detailed guidance for every stage of the campaign, downloadable files, news updates and opportunities for participating libraries to share ideas and collaborate.

Participating libraries also receive free printed materials to get started, such as stickers, bookmarks and posters. Full-color campaign handouts that provide the complete Geek the Library story are also included. Additional materials may be ordered for special events and activities.

Free field support is available for each local campaign with the focus on initial assistance with marketing strategies and launch. Beyond this point, field managers evaluate support needs on a case-by-case basis, and assistance may include phone calls, online conferences and on-site visits.

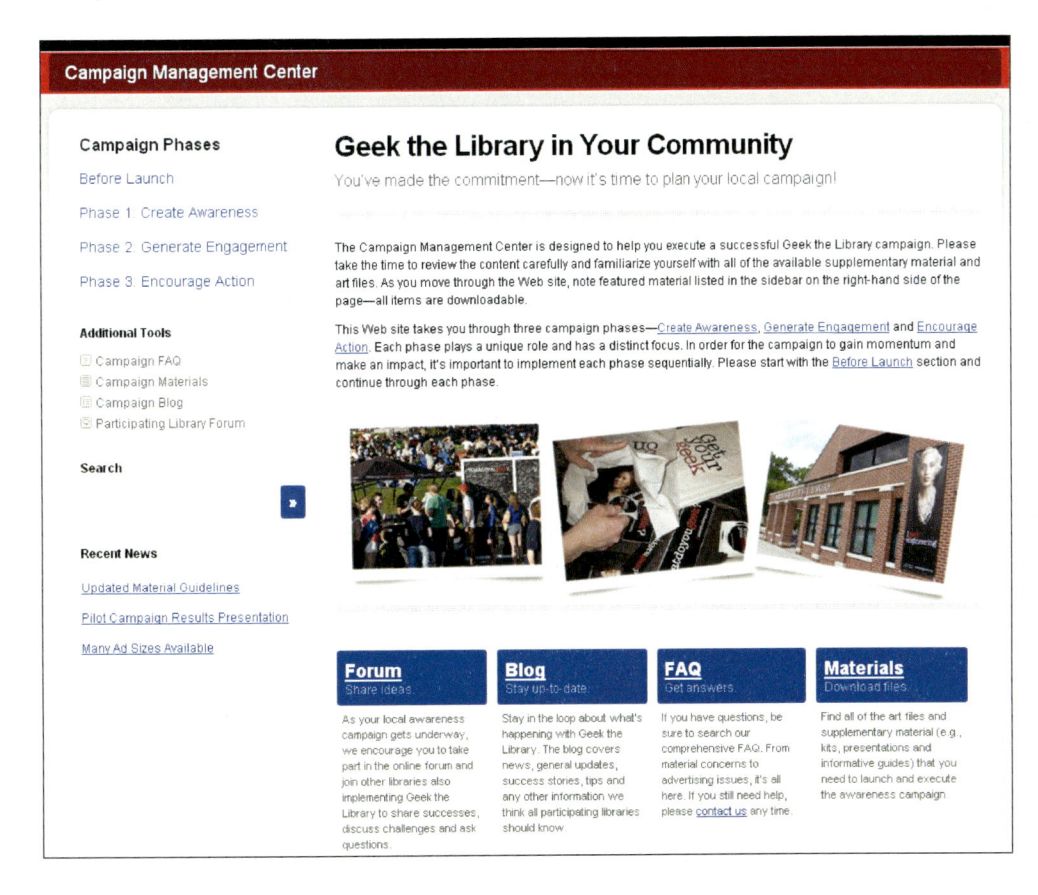

While any U.S. public library is encouraged to implement the campaign locally, it is important to consider the budget and staff resource commitment. Money for advertising, especially newspaper and magazine, is critical in building necessary campaign awareness. There are many opportunities available for discounted or inexpensive advertising—including partnering with other libraries in your area that are also adopting the program. Field managers can assist in developing an appropriate budget and getting the most out of every dollar.

The pilot findings demonstrate that advertising was a key element in building awareness in central Iowa and southern Georgia, but even libraries with small advertising budgets can be successful. The second group of pilot libraries, added after the initial launch in June 2009, had limited funds and found many creative ways to generate comparative awareness in their communities with unique combinations of marketing efforts (e.g., street lamp banners and taking part in local parades) that put less emphasis on paid advertising.

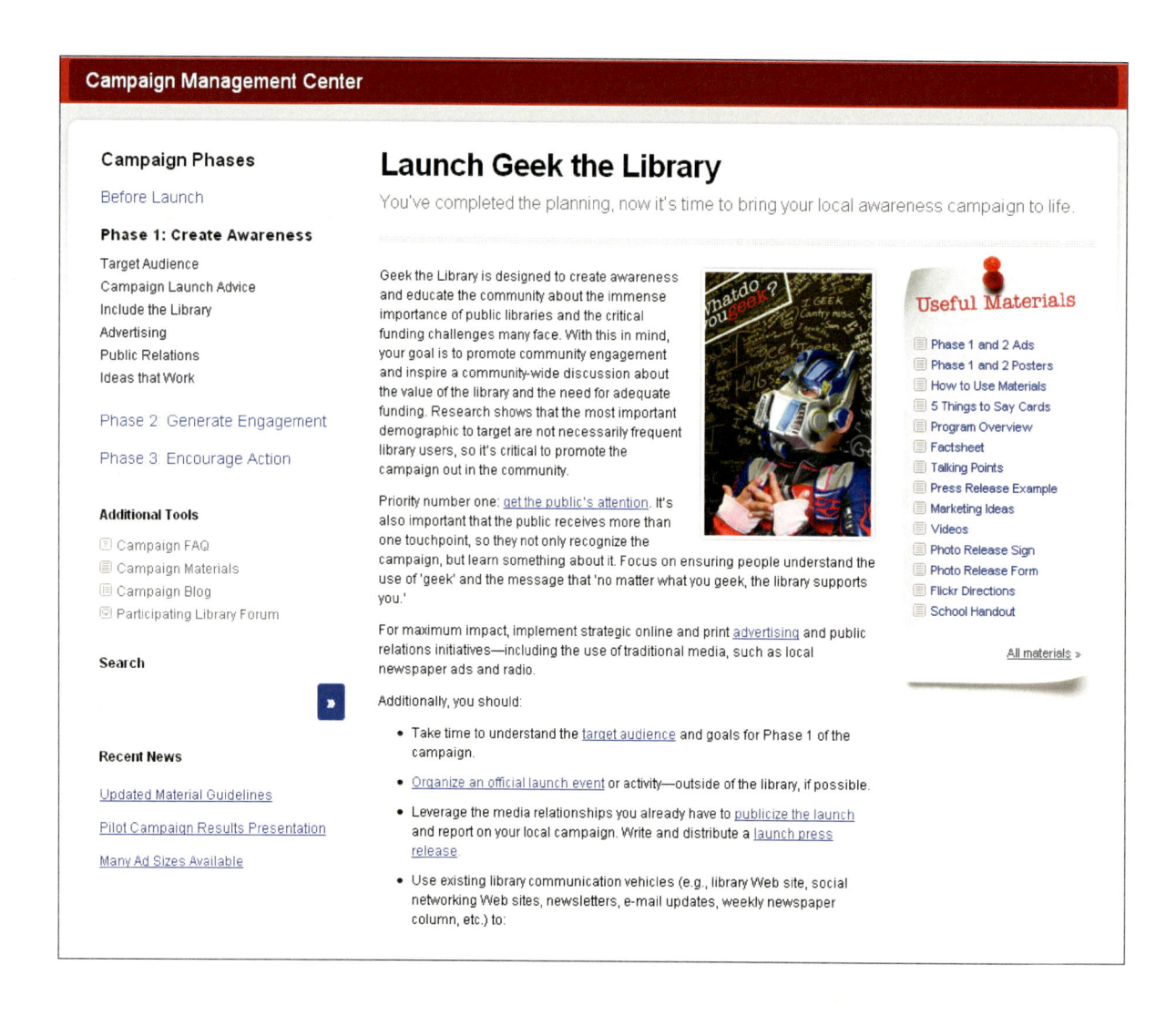

Campaign Management Center

Campaign Phases

Before Launch

Phase 1: Create Awareness
Target Audience
Campaign Launch Advice
Include the Library
Advertising
Public Relations
Ideas that Work

Phase 2: Generate Engagement

Phase 3: Encourage Action

Additional Tools
Campaign FAQ
Campaign Materials
Campaign Blog
Participating Library Forum

Search

Recent News
Updated Material Guidelines
Pilot Campaign Results Presentation
Many Ad Sizes Available

Launch Geek the Library

You've completed the planning, now it's time to bring your local awareness campaign to life.

Geek the Library is designed to create awareness and educate the community about the immense importance of public libraries and the critical funding challenges many face. With this in mind, your goal is to promote community engagement and inspire a community-wide discussion about the value of the library and the need for adequate funding. Research shows that the most important demographic to target are not necessarily frequent library users, so it's critical to promote the campaign out in the community.

Priority number one: get the public's attention. It's also important that the public receives more than one touchpoint, so they not only recognize the campaign, but learn something about it. Focus on ensuring people understand the use of 'geek' and the message that 'no matter what you geek, the library supports you.'

For maximum impact, implement strategic online and print advertising and public relations initiatives—including the use of traditional media, such as local newspaper ads and radio.

Additionally, you should:

- Take time to understand the target audience and goals for Phase 1 of the campaign.
- Organize an official launch event or activity—outside of the library, if possible.
- Leverage the media relationships you already have to publicize the launch and report on your local campaign. Write and distribute a launch press release.
- Use existing library communication vehicles (e.g., library Web site, social networking Web sites, newsletters, e-mail updates, weekly newspaper column, etc.) to:

Useful Materials
Phase 1 and 2 Ads
Phase 1 and 2 Posters
How to Use Materials
5 Things to Say Cards
Program Overview
Factsheet
Talking Points
Press Release Example
Marketing Ideas
Videos
Photo Release Sign
Photo Release Form
Flickr Directions
School Handout

All materials »

How Geek the Library works for your library ... top 10 list

1. It positions your library as vital to individuals and the community at large.

2. It serves as a reminder to the community that public library funding should not be taken for granted, and that the library is a critical public resource that helps people reeducate themselves, find jobs and transform their lives.

3. It helps debunk public library funding myths and reminds the public that the largest chunk of public library funding usually comes from local dollars.

4. It provides a lighthearted approach to encouraging critical conversations about your library's need for support and funding.

5. It creates opportunities to build important relationships with influential members of the community, and partner with community organizations, local businesses and schools, which will have value in long-term funding efforts.

6. It makes a full-scale and professionally designed awareness campaign simple to localize and execute.

7. It provides the materials and advice needed to cut through the marketing clutter and speak directly to the people who can provide the kind of support you need when it counts.

8. It provides an opportunity to be part of the events and activities where the public library may not be expected.

9. It builds advocacy and marketing skills that benefit the library well beyond the campaign.

10. It provides new and exciting ways to connect with your community and have fun.

Dedicated staff is key. Geek the Library is a community-based campaign—meaning the majority of promotional efforts should take place outside of the library. Having a consistent presence at local events, and developing media and community partnerships (with local businesses and schools, etc.) is necessary to effectively help the community learn about and make the connection between the campaign, the library and funding.

The most important commitment is the ability to demonstrate enthusiasm, embrace the bold look and feel of the campaign, and to have fun! This campaign is an opportunity to connect with your community like never before. Take advantage of it!

The need to successfully educate people about the library's important position within the community infrastructure and its transformational resources is at an all-time high, and will continue to be critical for many years to come. By doing so, this campaign has the potential to affect whether or not local communities increase library support now and in the future.

Geek the Library is a great opportunity for any public library to get its community talking about the library and start important local funding conversations.

Visit get.geekthelibrary.org for more information.

Glossary

Appendix A

Advocacy — Active support of a cause, idea or policy.

Barriers to Support — Second-lowest tier of the Library Supporter Segmentation Pyramid. Voters who, for a variety of reasons, have significant barriers to voting for increased library funding.

Bond/bond measure — An initiative to sell bonds for the purpose of acquiring funds for various public works projects.

Brand — The cumulative perceptions about an organization, company or product. A name, term, sign, symbol or design to identify a company, product or service.

Chronic Non Voters — Bottom tier of the Library Supporter Segmentation Pyramid. People who have not registered to vote or have a track record of choosing not to vote.

Creative concept — The core idea and framework of a marketing tactic or campaign.

Field manager — For the purpose of this report: An OCLC representative who helped Geek the Library pilot participants plan and execute the campaign.

Focus group — A form of qualitative research in which a group of people is asked about attitudes and opinions on a particular topic. Typically held in an interactive setting where participants are free to talk with other group members.

Geek — For the purpose of this report: To love, to enjoy, to celebrate, to have an intense passion for; to express interest in; to possess a large amount of knowledge in; to promote.

Geek board — A mobile board on which residents can write, or add in some other way, what they are passionate about.

Geek wall — A wall on which residents can write, or add in some other way, what they are passionate about.

Grassroots — A community-driven movement where activities are taken on by members of a group. These movements are often local.

Greater Good — Fifth segment of the Probable Supporters tier on the Library Supporter Segmentation Pyramid. Believes that the library plays an important role in serving the needs of the community and can be a great source of pride, given proper funding.

Just for Fun — First segment of the Probable Supporters tier on the Library Supporter Segmentation Pyramid. The heaviest users of the library, particularly of recreational activities and services.

Kid Driven — Second segment of the Probable Supporters tier on the Library Supporter Segmentation Pyramid. Willing to support the library financially because of the role it plays in educating and inspiring children.

Levy — An imposition of a tax.

Localization — For the purpose of this report: Combining local elements with awareness campaign components to ensure relevancy for local audiences.

Local public services — For the purpose of this report: The public library, fire department, police department, public health, public schools, road maintenance and park service.

Marketing campaign — A series of marketing programs sharing a specific goal and a unified theme.

Marketing tactics — Specific communications vehicles such as paid advertising (TV, radio, newspapers, billboards, direct mail, paid search), earned media (news stories, events, editorials) and social marketing (blogs, wikis, online outreach).

Market segmentation — Dividing a market into distinct groups of buyers on the basis of needs, characteristics or behaviors, who might require separate products or marketing mixes.

Media impression — A public relations term identifying the number of people who may have seen an article, heard something on the radio or in a podcast, watched something on TV or viewed something on a blog or Web site.

Paid media — Advertising (e.g., TV, radio, newspapers, billboards, direct mail, paid search) that includes sharing a brand message in a public space for a fee.

Pilot — A test or trial project to test the viability of a marketing campaign in specific markets for possible larger-scale dissemination.

Pilot library — For the purpose of this report: A small group of U.S. public libraries involved in the official Geek the Library pilot campaign.

Positioning — Arranging for a product to occupy a clear, distinctive and desirable place relative to competing products in the minds of target consumers.

Post-campaign — For the purpose of this report: Refers to any time after the official end of tracking and reporting of the Geek the Library pilot campaign in April 2010.

Post-wave — For the purpose of this report: Refers to the findings from the quantitative market research conducted in November 2009 in central Iowa and southern Georgia.

Pre-campaign — For the purpose of this report: Refers to any time prior to the Geek the Library pilot campaign launch in June 2009.

Pre-wave — For the purpose of this report: Refers to the findings from the quantitative market research conducted in central Iowa and southern Georgia prior to the Geek the Library pilot campaign launch in June 2009.

Probable Supporters — Voters who are likely to support library funding initiatives, yet are not fully committed.

Qualitative research — Qualitative research aims to gather an in-depth understanding of human behavior and the reasons that govern human behavior. Looks for the reasons behind various aspects of behavior, investigating the why and how of decision making, not just what, where and when.

Quantitative research — Quantitative research aims to investigate a human or social issue or behavior based on measurement with numbers and statistical analysis. The process of measurement is central to quantitative research because it provides the fundamental connection between empirical observation and mathematical expression of quantitative relationships.

Referendum — A direct vote in which an entire electorate is asked to accept or reject a particular proposal.

Super Supporters — People most firmly committed to supporting a library funding initiative.

List of Pilot Libraries

Appendix B

Georgia

Live Oak Public Libraries
  Bull Street Branch
  Carnegie Branch
  Effingham Branch
  Forest City Branch
  Islands Branch
  Kayton Branch
  Liberty Branch
  Midway-Riceboro Branch
  Ogeechee Branch
  Oglethorpe Mall Branch
  Ola Wyeth Branch
  Port City Branch
  Port Wentworth Branch
  South Effingham Branch
  Southwest Chatham Branch
  Thunderbolt Branch
  Tybee Island Branch
  West Broad Branch
  West Chatham Branch
  W.W. Law Branch

Ohoopee Regional Library System
  Glennville Public Library
  Ladson Genealogical Library
  Montgomery County Library
  Nelle Brown Memorial Library
  Tattnall County Library
  Vidalia-Toombs County Library

Okefenokee Regional Library System
  Alma-Bacon County Public Library
  Appling County Public Library

Piedmont Regional Library System
  Auburn Public Library
  Banks County Public Library
  Braselton Library
  Commerce Public Library
  Harold S. Swindle Public Library
  Jefferson Public Library
  Maysville Public Library
  Pendergrass Public Library
  Statham Public Library
  Talmo Public Library
  Winder Library

Satilla Regional Library System
  Jeff Davis Public Library

Screven-Jenkins Regional Library System
  Screven County Library

Statesboro Regional Library System
  Candler County Library
  Evans County Library
  Pembroke Library
  Richmond Hill Public Library
  Statesboro Regional Library

Three Rivers Regional Library System
  Hog Hammock Public Library
  Ida Hilton Public Library
  Long County Public Library
  Wayne County Library

Illinois

Zion-Benton Public Library

Indiana

Shelbyville-Shelby County Public Library

Iowa

Adel Public Library
Altoona Public Library
Ames Public Library
Bertha Bartlett Public Library
Bondurant Community Library
Cambridge Memorial Public Library
Carlisle Public Library
Clive Public Library
Collins Public Library
Colo Public Library
Des Moines Public Library
   Central Library
   East Side Branch
   Forest Avenue Branch
   Franklin Avenue Branch
   Northside Branch
   South Side Branch

DeSoto Public Library
Dexter Public Library
Granger Public Library
Grimes Public Library
Huxley Public Library
Indianola Public Library
Johnston Public Library
Kirkendall Public Library
Lacona Public Library
Linden Public Library
Maxwell Public Library
Milo Public Library
Minburn Public Library
Mitchellville Public Library
Nevada Public Library
Norwalk Public Library
Perry Public Library
Pleasant Hill Public Library
Polk City Community Library
Redfield Public Library
Roland Public Library
Roy R. Estle Memorial Library
Runnells Public Library
Slater Public Library
Urbandale Public Library
Van Meter Public Library
Waukee Public Library
West Des Moines Public Library
Woodward Public Library
Zearing Public Library

Wisconsin

Milwaukee Public Library

About Our Partners

Appendix C

Bill & Melinda Gates Foundation

Guided by the belief that every life has equal value, the Bill & Melinda Gates Foundation works to help all people lead healthy, productive lives. In developing countries, it focuses on improving people's health and giving them the chance to lift themselves out of hunger and extreme poverty. In the United States, it seeks to ensure that all people—especially those with the fewest resources—have access to the opportunities they need to succeed in school and life. Based in Seattle, Washington, the foundation is led by CEO Jeff Raikes and Co-chair William H. Gates Sr., under the direction of Bill and Melinda Gates and Warren Buffett. Learn more at www.gatesfoundation.org.

Leo Burnett USA

Leo Burnett USA, comprising the Leo Burnett brand agency and marketing partner Arc Worldwide, is one of the world's largest agency networks and a subsidiary of Publicis Groupe, the world's fourth-largest communications company. Leo Burnett holds people at the center of its strategic thinking, technological innovation and creative ideas, focusing first and foremost on human behavior before attempting to tell a brand's story. At the core of understanding human insight is Leo Burnett's own quantitative Research Services group. This group is integral to the strategic team and is responsible for handling all types of custom quantitative market research, providing upfront insights into human behavior—the foundation for Burnett's brand work. With this approach, Leo Burnett ensures that people who buy into client brands believe in them all the more. With expertise in mass advertising and digital, promotional and retail marketing, Leo Burnett partners with blue-chip clients such as The Coca-Cola Company, Diageo, Kellogg, McDonald's, Procter & Gamble and Samsung. Learn more at www.leoburnett.com.

About OCLC

Appendix D

OCLC

Founded in 1967 and headquartered in Dublin, Ohio, OCLC is a nonprofit library service and research organization that has provided computer-based cataloging, reference, resource sharing, eContent, preservation, library management and Web services to 72,000 libraries in 170 countries and territories. OCLC and its member libraries worldwide have created and maintain WorldCat, the world's richest online resource for finding library materials. Search WorldCat.org on the Web at www.worldcat.org.

OCLC advocacy programs are part of a long-term initiative to champion libraries to increase their visibility and viability within their communities. Programs include advertising and marketing materials to reinforce the idea of the library as relevant, and market research reports that identify and communicate trends of importance to the library profession. For more information, visit www.oclc.org.